# Special Praise for *Fear: Feel It, Face It, and Grow*

"Whether you spend time in the rooms of a twelve-step fellowship or have wondered what can be gained through such a recovery program, Mark Edick offers a rich compendium of learning in *Fear: Feel It, Face, It, and Grow*. With his thoughtful voice of recovery that is full of wisdom, honesty, humor, and hope, Mark helps readers see constructive ways to honor their fears and to live and work with them in order to have a life with more freedom, strength, and serenity. Readers will benefit tremendously from Mark's self-awareness that is ever-present, as well as his loving and meaningful relationship with his sponsor. The learning that Mark offers extends way beyond not drinking or using. As Mark says, 'the things I've learned aren't just life-savers; they are life-creators.' I agree."

**Nancy L. Johnston, MS, LPC, LSATP**
**Author of** *Disentangle: When You've*
*Lost Your Self in Someone Else*

"When you live your life in fear, every day can be the hardest place in the world to be, but it doesn't have to be this way. No one knows this better than author Mark Edick. Drawing on his own experience, as well as the experience of others, Mark openly discusses how fear was a significant part of his life and how he learned to cope with the complexity of fear. Mark gathers his experiences in recovery and gives hope to those who feel anxious, depressed, and fearful and gives them strength to continue onward and to see what they have to look forward to when they get to the other side."

**Catherine Kania, LMSW, ACSW**
**Mental Health Therapist**

"In his second book in the recovery genre, author Mark Edick offers a colloquy, a meditation, a reflection, a deeply personal negotiation with the emotion of fear. So what's keeping you from reading? Could it be fear?"

**Michael Stratton, LCSW**

**Fear:** Feel It, Face It, and Grow

# FEAR

Feel It, Face It, and Grow

**Mark Edick**

CENTRAL RECOVERY PRESS

CENTRAL RECOVERY PRESS

Central Recovery Press (CRP) is committed to publishing exceptional materials addressing addiction treatment, recovery, and behavioral healthcare, including original and quality books, audio/visual communications, and Web-based new media. Through a diverse selection of titles, we seek to contribute to a broad range of unique resources for professionals, recovering individuals and their families, and the general public.

For more information, visit **www.centralrecoverypress.com**

Central Recovery Press, Las Vegas, NV 89129

© 2012 by Utopia Bookworks, Inc. All rights reserved. Published 2012. Printed in the United States of America.

Publisher:   Central Recovery Press
             3321 N. Buffalo Drive
             Las Vegas, NV 89129

17 16 15 14 13 12   1 2 3 4 5

**ISBN-13**: 978-1-936290-72-7 (trade paper)
**ISBN-10**: 1-936290-72-3
**ISBN-13**: 978-1-936290-85-7 (e-book)
**ISBN-10**: 1-936290-85-5

Brief excerpts from *Alcoholics Anonymous* are reprinted with permission of Alcoholics Anonymous World Services, Inc. ("AAWS"). Permission to reprint this material does not mean that AAWS has reviewed or approved the contents of this publication, or that AAWS necessarily agrees with the views expressed herein. AA is a program of recovery from alcoholism only—use of the Twelve Steps in connection with programs and activities that are patterned after AA, but which address other problems, or in any other non-AA context, does not imply otherwise.

**Publisher's Note:** This is a memoir; a work based on fact recorded to the best of the author's memory. Central Recovery Press books represent the experiences and opinions of their authors only. Every effort has been made to ensure that events, institutions, and statistics presented in our books as facts are accurate and up-to-date. To protect their privacy, the names of some of the people and institutions in this book have been changed.

**Book design by David Leicester Hardy**

# Dedication

To Miss Vivian Costello, who always gave more than she took and left the world a better place than she found it.

To Don Walter, who stepped into a big pair of shoes and didn't care if he filled them. One of the things I admire about him most is his ability to be himself.

# Acknowledgments

To all the people—in recovery and not—who have helped me learn and grow in my own life, especially those who have helped me through or pushed me through my walls of fear. I thank you all for your help in my personal growth and on my spiritual path.

To my publisher, Central Recovery Press, for putting forth the effort to make this book available to anyone who might find it helpful in his or her own personal and spiritual growth. I thank you more than you know for helping me help others.

I would like to thank my editor, Daniel Kaelin, for his tireless work and support in bringing this book to completion. I could not have done it without him.

Finally, I thank God for the opportunity to share what I have been given.

# Contents

Acknowledgments ................................................. IX

Introduction ........................................................ XIII

01 | Fear: Breaking It Down ............................................ 1

02 | Anger and Depression ............................................ 25

03 | The Learning Experience ........................................ 45

04 | Thinking It Through .............................................. 62

05 | Getting Honest ..................................................... 78

06 | Expectations, Emotions, Experience, and Ego ........... 94

07 | Time and Worry .................................................. 118

08 | Faith ................................................................. 130

09 | Happiness .......................................................... 140

10 | Patience, Practice, Problems, and Principles ........... 156

11 | Giving, Living, Gratitude, and Growth ................... 180

# Introduction

Fear is something we deal with every day. Sometimes it's a large, debilitating giant; other times it's so small as to go almost unnoticed. Yet fear follows us nearly everywhere we go. Some fears we can avoid for the most part, like being afraid of snakes or of flying. Others we must face whether we want to or not, like our first job interview.

Fear controlled my life for so long, driving me in the wrong direction— or at least it kept me from going in the right direction. When I got into recovery and discovered how much impact it had on my life, I decided I had to do something about it. When I began to look at my fear and discovered the extent to which it ran my life and was a part of my being, I decided I had to learn to deal with it in a more positive manner.

As I looked back over my life, I found that I had never really dealt with fear on a conscious level. I had simply let it have its way with me, attempting to move through it only when I wanted, or needed, something very badly. As I was making this discovery, I noticed some common threads with which fear worked in my life.

The level of fear I felt had to do with my familiarity with the task at hand. It seems that the first time I try something, fear can shake me to my foundation. While doing my first jigsaw puzzle wasn't too traumatic, getting my first job was, as was asking a girl out on a date for the first time. After getting the job or getting the date, my life seemed to smooth out and the fear subsided.

While familiarity can lessen the amount of fear that I feel, in some instances it never seems to go away altogether. I have spoken publicly on many occasions since I began my recovery. Even though I can give a speech today without much discomfort, the first several I gave were nerve-wracking. Although I am much more comfortable speaking in public these days, I still get nervous before I speak. No matter how well I know the topic or how prepared I am, I still get butterflies in my stomach. I have found this to be a natural, normal part of the process of public speaking.

Another factor that plays a part in the level of fear I feel seems to depend upon how badly I want or need whatever it is that I am going after—or, should I say, how much I have convinced myself that I want or need it. Even though it is easier for me to ask a woman out on a date these days, the greater my desire to spend time with her, the more difficult it is for me to ask.

I remember when I really wanted a job—my second full-time job. It would pay very well, and even though I was a nervous wreck when I started the job, I eventually made it a career. The amazing thing is that today I can see that I kept that job because I was afraid I couldn't replace the income it provided with my level of education at that time. I let fear convince me that I couldn't do any better. That may have been true because all I had at the time was a high school education; I understand now that I could have gone back to school. Fear made me lazy by convincing me that I couldn't get through college. Real or imagined, fear is fear. It works on me by eroding my life—*if I let it.*

While some people say that there are irrational fears—like my fear of not being able to find a better job—I never try to tell anyone that the fear they feel is not rational. After all, it is rational to them, at least for the time being. Until they expose themselves to the fear and move through it repeatedly, until they come to see the truth, their fear will remain rational and very real to them.

I just call it working my way through the fear. I wrote this book to show others how I learned to work my way through the fears I find in my life today. It is my desire to share what I have learned that makes me want to do this, because what works for me can also work for you. I'm not a clinician, but I am speaking from my own experience. My experience tells me that I need to keep it as simple as I can when it comes to something as complicated and pervasive as fear.

Today I see two major characteristics of my fear. The first characteristic is that it wears many faces and changes them as often as it needs to in order to keep me off balance. The second is that it follows me around all the time, waiting for the opportunity to pounce on me like a lion on a mouse.

Since I have found a way to deal with my fear today, and since I don't see it packing its bags and leaving anytime soon, I have decided to look at fear as just a part of the process, of any process, including the process of life.

While I don't mean to try to diminish the impact of fear by saying it is just part of the process, what I do intend to do is cut it down to size in my head and in my life. My hope is that you too will come to see fear as just part of the process of everyday life.

Like many things in life, we know fear isn't going away; we know it keeps us from doing things we want to do; we know it makes us nervous, sweaty, and uncomfortable.

Now let's take a look at how we can learn to take this monster and make friends with it, or at least shake hands with it and become more comfortable with each other.

Let's take a look at "the man behind the curtain," see him for what he is, and deal with him as just another part of the process of living a happy, productive life, a life where we turn fear from a debilitating monster into a tool we can use to our advantage.

When it comes to fear, I think the best thing to do is to *feel it, face it, and grow.*

# 01 | Fear: Breaking It Down

I used for many years because of fear. It ran my life like a drill sergeant at boot camp. I did what it told me to do, and I did it for so long that it became my nature. Generally, it told me to run. "Run away from what scares you" is what fear whispered into my ear. Since running was what I did most, I became really good at it. They say that fight or flight are the two main responses to fear. I chose flight so often that I'm surprised I didn't turn into an airplane. Flight became my only mode of dealing with fear. The more I ran, the stronger my fear grew, and often because of the simplest of things. Soon I became afraid of more and more things. Eventually I was living in a state of near-constant paranoia; I was running from everything in my life, and I didn't deal with much of anything.

For years I had so many fears running my life that I didn't know which way to turn, so I turned to alcohol and drugs to help me not to feel the fear.

It worked for a while. In fact, it worked right up until it quit working; but by that time, it was too late. My friends (alcohol and drugs) had not only abandoned me, but had turned on me. When I reached this point, I was not only full of fear, but I couldn't stop drinking and drugging, either. While I choose not to blame fear for my drinking and drugging, I have discovered that the fear was there long before I began abusing alcohol and drugs.

One of my biggest fears during my younger years was women. The more attractive they were, the more I wanted them, and the more fear I felt. It began so long ago, I could actually say it was a fear of girls. Two instances come to mind of my ability to deal or to not deal with my fear of girls while I was in high school.

When I was fourteen, I fell madly in love with my best friend's sister. She was about three years older than I was, and she graduated during my freshman year. I never saw her at school because we were on split shifts—the juniors and seniors went to school in the morning and the freshmen and sophomores went in the afternoon—but I hung out with her younger brother, so none of that mattered. I still saw her often, and as I now look back, I think it was clear to anyone watching, that I was crazy about her. And she knew it too! Halfway through my freshman year I told her that when I got my driver's license, I would take her out for dinner and a movie. Her reply was simple. She said, "That sounds like fun." Little did I know that I would never muster the courage to follow through with my promise. Even though I knew she would go out with me, when I got my license I simply couldn't gather the nerve to actually ask her out. Fear dictated that I mustn't follow through on this promise. It was only the beginning of the many opportunities I would miss in my life thanks to having this selfish, manipulative, controlling entity running the show.

While in high school there was another girl, a girl I graduated with, who grabbed my attention. She was homecoming queen, prom queen, and, of course, one of the most popular girls in school. I idolized her from afar; to approach her would have been too much.

To this day, I occasionally wonder what life might have been like if I had acted on either one of these desires. For many years—all through my drinking days, as I remember them—I relived these dreams with regret and remorse. Today I find a fondness has replaced the regret in these daydreams. I no longer wish I had done things differently. I simply enjoy the feeling of love I had for those two women as I let the daydream of what life might have been like play across my mind. While I reminisce, I wish them all the best. Of course, I have come a long way from those fear-filled days of yesteryear, but those were the days when my drinking and drugging began.

For the longest time, drinking gave me a sense of courage. It was never enough to do the things I really wanted to do—like ask one of those girls out on a date—but it was usually enough to get me to do other things or ask out other girls, ones who didn't intimidate me quite as much. Alcohol and drugs are like that: they provide courage while at the same time tilting the brain into thinking things through in a far-from-rational manner. This often leads to doing silly, crazy, or just plain stupid things. I believe it is just this kind of thing that led to the joke that goes something like this: "What are an alcoholic's famous last words? 'Hold my beer and watch this.'"

I am relatively certain that fear made it impossible for me to feel normal or to feel like I fit in with the rest of the kids my age. I know fear played a role in keeping me from doing many things I wanted to do. I also believe it kept me from making friends I wanted to make—I had a small number of friends growing up—and from attempting to do some of the things I would have liked to do. I did try out for sports, but I didn't do well thanks to my lack of ability in certain sports. Some of my coaches detested me due to the erratic behavior caused by my drinking and drugging.

I was told in sixth grade that I should make a career of singing, but I didn't pursue it, or any of the other performing arts, thanks to my fear of being labeled in a derogatory way. After all, I began taking ballet at the age of eleven, and others told me during the following years that I should make a career of that, too. That was enough ammunition for those who knew about my dancing, without me adding to the mix. Fear convinced me to avoid this field of endeavor.

Fear changed the way I felt about myself, as well as how I felt about the people around me. I had it in my fearful mind that teachers were out to cause me trouble when they were really trying to help me learn. Any authority figure was cause for alarm: police, teachers, doctors, and adults in general drove my fear to great heights. Although I see now how irrational my fear was, it caused me great pain while I was growing up, and continued into my adult life. In fact, when I finally got into recovery I discovered that I had to find a way to deal with it. Running was no longer an option if I wanted to live a full and normal life.

Fear drove the choices I made, and those choices led to consequences. Since I made most of my choices based on fear, most of my consequences were of a negative nature. I even came to believe that consequences were always a negative thing, as in "If you do that you will *suffer* the consequences." I thought that I always had to suffer *through* consequences. My thinking has changed in this area thanks to what I have learned in recovery, but for most of my life I did my best to lessen the impact of consequences rather than simply do things that would bring positive consequences into my life.

## A More Positive Look at Fear

Fear is part of life. In fact, life might be boring without it. However, fear can also disrupt my life in many ways. I can let it stop me from doing things I want to do, make me do things I don't want to do, and generally wreak havoc in my day-to-day life. Fear can also cost me friendships through my not pursuing them or by causing me or the other person to end the relationship. Yes, fear can be an enemy, an often inevitable and invisible enemy.

I think anyone would agree that fear is a part of life and that it isn't going to leave us anytime soon—probably never, and "never is a long time," as my dad likes to say. If fear isn't going to go away, the question becomes "How can I live with the fear that slithers through me from day to day?" The best answer, as usual, is simple. It is simple to say, yet difficult to do—at least at first—although it does get easier with practice. The answer is to deal with it head-on.

Like anything else, fear isn't something that can be dealt with without some effort. Just as we have to learn to deal with new challenges, we can learn to deal with fear in either positive or negative ways, ways that either help or harm us. If we choose to deal with the fear instead of just reacting to it, we can learn to use it. If we choose to take positive action when fear shows its ugly head instead of hiding from it, we can make genuine progress. The key to dealing with fear in a positive manner is first to recognize it for what it is. I must understand that I am feeling fear, rather than simply let my emotions drive me. If I don't acknowledge the fear, I may never get a grip on the matter.

In Franklin D. Roosevelt's inaugural address, given on March 4, 1933, he mentioned fear. Most people are familiar with the quotation, "The only thing we have to fear is fear itself." However, that is only a portion of a sentence, which is only part of his speech. One might argue that it is taken out of context. I won't argue that point here. I would like to look at the entire sentence, though. Here it is: "So first of all let me assert my firm belief that the only thing we have to fear is fear itself—nameless, unreasoning, unjustified terror which paralyzes needed efforts to convert retreat into advance."

Now that says something. Not that the shorter quote doesn't; it does, just not as much. I have done some thinking on the shorter version of the quote and have brought meaning from it into my life, because, when it comes to fear, I think I should be afraid of letting it run my life. I've spent far too much of my life living in fear—letting my anxieties dictate what I could or couldn't do, what I should or shouldn't do, whom I should befriend and whom I should avoid, or at least not befriend, what kind of job I should have. I've stayed in a job I didn't like because fear told me I'd never find another one, let alone a better one. For many years I didn't look to see if there might be a better job, because fear told me I had to quit one job before I could look for another one, and I believed that conniving, life-wrecking fear. Looking back, I think I chose to believe that particular fear because it seemed easier than not believing it. It seemed easier to stay in a rut than to take a critical look at why I was staying in the rut.

When I finally began looking at fear instead of just retreating from it, I began to see just how much I let fear run my life. I had to allow fear to take the lead. It couldn't do so without my consent. While most of the time I didn't consciously give my consent, I didn't exactly protest its control, either; I simply reacted to life, and to fear. When I did protest, I usually did so while "the committee" discussed it in my mind, instead of my discussing it with a trusted friend. A friend might be able to shed some light on the matter, which could help me see things as they really are instead of through the unfocused and blurred lens of fear. Fear likes to keep me in the dark recesses of my own mind where I can't see my options; however, when fear is exposed to the spotlight of truth, it usually begins to fade, shrink, or disappear altogether. The truth about fear is that it's just as afraid of me as I am of it, but we'll discuss that a little bit later.

Let's look at the second half of the quotation from FDR: "nameless, unreasoning, unjustified terror, which paralyzes needed efforts to convert retreat into advance." To me, that is a wonderful definition of what fear really is. FDR's understanding of fear is not what the dictionary says *exactly*, but it captures the meaning of fear for me today. Another way to look at it is to define it in this way: "fear: [a] nameless, unreasoning, unjustified terror, which paralyzes needed efforts to convert retreat into advance." If that doesn't describe fear, I don't know what does. Fear is often nameless, and nearly always unreasoning. It's usually unjustified, though I like to justify it because it seems like fear can provide me with an easy way out. Fear can quickly paralyze my efforts to convert retreat or hiding into advance or taking necessary action, whether I justify it or not. The question then becomes "How do I deal with this menace?" The answer, again, is simple, but not so easy.

I must face my fears head-on.

I used to believe that overcoming fear meant that I was supposed to be fearless, that I was supposed to find a way not to feel afraid. This is just plain wrong. "Don't be afraid" is misguided advice. It can't be done. If I wait until I stop feeling fear, I'll never do anything. I've found that I can't make fear leave by thinking or wishing it away—no matter how hard I try. To rid myself of fear I must walk through it, repeatedly walk through it. I don't remember ever being told this directly. Instead, I learned it by doing. My sponsor repeatedly pushed me through "walls of fear" until I concluded that fear is overcome not through willpower or wishing it away, but through courageous action.

Courageous action is something I've also had to redefine, because my definition of courage used to be "the absence of fear." I thought that in order to be courageous, I had to rid myself of fear. My experience and subsequent research have led me to a new understanding of what courage is and what it is not. Courage is not the absence of fear, because courageous people are afraid too!

Courage is taking action—doing the right thing, or the thing I want or need to do—even though I'm afraid to do so. Courage is staring fear in the face and moving forward, toward it, not away from it. Courage is walking through that wall of fear.

I've seen fear as a "wall" because a wall will stop, or at least slow, my progress toward a goal. And fear operates like that wall. Whatever the goal, it is insignificant as far as fear is concerned. Fear's objective is to stop progress—to turn advance into retreat. The way it accomplishes this is by convincing me, through intimidation, threat, or coercion that I will fail to make the desired progress, and that I will make a fool of myself in some way. Because of this, I must seek out and get to know my fears. I must consciously decide to do things of which I am afraid. I must do this on a consistent basis. I must not allow success or failure to be too large a part of the equation, because if I attempt to do something I am afraid of, I usually succeed. Even if I do not attain the results I desire, the attempt is a success because I faced my fear. The truth is that the outcome is often not my decision anyway. I am required only to make the attempt and to do my best, and then let God take care of the results. I am in the *action business* and God is in the *results business*. If the outcome is not to my liking, I can try again. I must remember that failure is a teacher; failure is a beginning; failure is not the end. I am not a failure if God provides a result that is not of my choosing. That is His business, His job, and listening to my fear is one way of telling God what I think the results—His results—should be. I am not God, but I sometimes need a gentle reminder of that. One of the easiest ways I have found to face my fear is to take a good, hard look at what I really fear. Some may say, "That sounds simple," but it really is more complicated than that, because fear is an insidious force. Fear wants me to think I am afraid of something large, something that I cannot overcome. The truth is that fear is smaller than it appears. Fear somehow has the ability to appear much larger than it really is.

I had a friend who was thinking of moving to South Carolina. Most of her family lived there and she wanted to be closer to them. However, she was afraid to make the move. She began telling me about her fears. She is legally blind, and for her, just getting around can be a challenge. She was used to her present, familiar surroundings, and was afraid that she might not be able to find a living situation where transportation would be as accessible as it was where she lived. She had a good job and was afraid she might not be able to find one to replace it. She was afraid of the actual move; she was afraid of how she would get everything packed and moved to South Carolina. Her list went on. If you use your imagination just a little, I am sure you can come up with a few fears you might have of moving five states away.

I suggested to her that she write her fears on a piece of paper. I suggested she put her fears in a tangible form she could evaluate objectively. I had never done this myself; in fact, the idea had never occurred to me, but it sounded like a good idea. I felt certain the idea had come from God, since it didn't come from me, only through me, and I had never tried it myself; yet it sounded sensible. I told her I had never tried this myself, but that I thought it might just help her to see her fear for what it really was. She took this advice and wrote down all the things she was afraid of about her upcoming move. Six months later, she was living in South Carolina.

A few months after she successfully faced her fears and moved to South Carolina, I had the opportunity to put this method of facing fears to good use. A wonderful opportunity to organize a hotline in my town emerged. Yet I was paralyzed by the fear. I had run my mouth—as I sometimes do—about how we should provide a twenty-four-hour hotline manned by volunteers who were in recovery instead of paying a professional answering service whose employees had no experience in recovery. I suddenly had the job of making it happen. My first thought was that I had opened my mouth and inserted my foot. Then, when the fear set in ferociously and I wanted to back out, I remembered the suggestion I had given my friend regarding her fear about moving. I made a list of my fears.

I was afraid people would not sign up to do the work, or that the whole thing would be a flop; I would fail miserably, or people would sign up and then not show up to work their shift.

I wouldn't have enough bright ideas to get the hotline going, and I wouldn't get the help I needed.

I wrote down these fears and more. Then I took a good, hard look at them. The fears really boiled down to two types: fear of what other people might think of me (especially if I failed), and fear of not being in control. If I failed, I feared people would judge me negatively. Since I could not control the situation—it was beyond my ability—I had fears about all the things I could not control.

Seeing my fears for what they were, I did what I could do. For the most part that consisted of making a schedule, printing some flyers, and asking for help getting the word out that we needed volunteers. Then I started working phone shifts—pretty much all the shifts that were not covered by volunteers. Oh, and I prayed. I prayed for help and I prayed for courage.

Well, things worked out. We now have our phones manned twenty-four hours a day by people in recovery. I was able to face the fear by writing it down and taking a good look at what it was that I really feared. When I did that, my fears looked small, even silly, and as I look back on my part in the whole thing, I see that what I did was one person's part. I did what I could. The key to success in this case was that eighty-plus other people did what they could too; they continue to do what they can to make the hotline the success it is today. I left my role as chairperson some time ago, and others have taken over the chairperson's position. They have added new ideas, which have made things even better. However, the volunteers make the whole thing happen. They do the real work. I was happy to do my part, despite my fears, to get the ball rolling. Probably the greatest lesson I learned from the entire experience is the value of writing down my fears. Once I wrote them down, I could see them for their silliness. I continue this practice today, and I plan to do so for the rest of my days. When I find my fears holding me back, I write them down. Then I look at them until I see them for what they really are. Once I see the truth, my fear begins to dissolve and I am able to summon the courage to do my part. I am also willing to let other people do their part.

Today I see fear as an overinflated bully who needs only a good, hard look to be seen for who he really is. When I take the time to see through my fears—to see them for what they really are—I find it is not too difficult to summon the courage necessary to walk through the walls they represent. The more often I do the exercise, the easier it gets to repeat the process. As I practice overcoming fear, accomplishing the task gets a little bit easier. When I stop feeding fear, it begins to die a slow death. While it will most likely never die completely, it does weaken as I feed my courage and become even stronger.

## Multiplying Fear

There are so many things to fear. It is no wonder fears multiply when I keep them bottled up in my head. The same fear can manifest itself in many ways: failure, success, not knowing how to do something, getting hurt, hurting someone else; the list is nearly endless. Yet I've been able to boil all my anxieties down to five root causes by taking a serious, critical look at them. My personal fears are these five:

- Fear of failing.
- Fear of what other people will think of me.
- Fear of losing control.
- Fear of not getting something I want.
- Fear of losing something I have.

With work, I can boil them down to just the last two—fear of not getting what I want and fear of losing something I have. Fear of failing includes my fear of success. While that may sound odd on the surface, it is true, because if I succeed at something I'll be expected to follow that up with more success— even if I am the only one to have this unreasonable expectation. When I do something and succeed, or have what I consider a successful outcome, I automatically reset my expectations to this new level. While this isn't always true, I've found it to be true often enough to make it my rule. For example, if I'm asked to give a speech on a subject I'm familiar with, though I do not consider myself much of a public speaker, I can still walk through the fear and give the speech because I'm familiar with the subject matter. Once I've given the speech, I will have a new level of expectation for myself when it comes to public speaking: I will expect that I can do it again next time. However, if I'm asked to speak again, the subject matter may be something I'm not familiar with. What will I do then? This is fear of failure mixed with fear of what other people will think of me—and I haven't even been asked to give the second speech yet. This fear can affect my first speech, since my mind will likely preoccupy itself with what others may think at some time before I give the speech, and this fear of what other people will think of me can paralyze me. Yet I don't even have an idea what those people really think.

In the end, I'm the one doing the thinking. When it comes to thinking, it's important for me to remember that I'm the only one doing my thinking. This is the main reason my sponsor told me, "It's none of your business what other people think of you."

I'll never be able to please everyone, so I need to stop worrying about it. There is a great sense of freedom in knowing that.

The sense of freedom I gain lets me see that it isn't what other people think about me, it's what I think they think of me that has the power to hurt me. After all, most people don't come up and tell me what they think of me, especially if it is negative. Nearly all the negative things people think of me are not my reality, but exist only in my own vivid imagination. I make these thoughts and fears up as I go along. And I make up other fears that accompany the original fears I imagined. Then, I project these fears onto the other person or people, even though there is a strong possibility these people weren't thinking of me at all. It is only logical. Many people practice "projection," or the attribution of their own thoughts, feelings, and conclusions to others.

To prove my point, let's look at an example of what other people thought of me, or so I thought, when I took on the job of establishing a volunteer helpline. The only people who ever told me what they thought of what I did with the helpline were the people who thought I did something positive. While there were probably people who thought I did it for a selfish or some other negative reason, they never told me their thoughts on the subject. Truth be told, most people—even the ones who knew I was behind the revamping of the system (and there weren't that many of them to begin with)—probably never gave it much thought at all. If they did, they kept their thoughts to themselves, because I never heard about it.

Therefore, if I thought they harbored ill feeling toward me, it was my own thoughts I was battling, not theirs. If I look at this situation under the spotlight of reason, as opposed to the darkness of my irrationality, I will see it for what it is. When I say, "I think Sam doesn't like me," all I have to do is stop after the first two words in the sentence to know who is doing the thinking. I am. "I think Sam doesn't like me." Sam hasn't made a comment regarding the matter, but I have assigned him the role of not liking me because it fits into my fearful way of thinking.

Even if I happen to be right, and Sam doesn't like me, what should that matter? Sam is one person. I know I can't please everyone, so Sam now falls into the category of people I couldn't or didn't please this time around. Maybe Sam has a good reason for not liking me, but that shouldn't matter since Sam's reasons are just that—his reasons. If Sam doesn't like the idea that I revamped the helpline, maybe it is because he secretly wishes he had done so himself. The reason shouldn't matter, and I need to get to where it doesn't matter to me.

If Sam doesn't like it, that is his problem, not mine. If at some point Sam makes it known to me that he doesn't like what I did, I need to let him own his problem. Even though fear tells me I need to fix it, I don't need to take on Sam's problem or problems. Yet I've been known to do just that. If I have a problem with the way people treat me or the things they tell me, I sometimes allow fear to tell me that I need to fix the problem even though it may be outside my control to do so. Somewhere in the mess, I take my problem of wanting them to like me and twist it in such a way so that I think it is the other person's responsibility to fix it, when it is still my problem. My problem is still with Sam. I want Sam to like me, even though he probably won't. I can't change Sam. I can only change myself and how I allow my perceptions to affect me.

I change the way I perceive things by changing the way I talk to myself.

Have you ever said something like "I have a problem with Sam," either out loud or to yourself? I'll bet you have. I know I have. When I say something like that, my tendency is to think that Sam is the one with the problem or that Sam is the one who needs to change. However, if I look at what I'm saying, I'll see the truth. "I have a problem with Sam" really means that I'm the one with the problem.

If I reverse this perception, which is what I need to do if Sam has a problem with me, I find that Sam is the one with the problem.

You can look at this in two ways: "Sam has a problem with me," or "I think Sam doesn't like me." The first way of looking at the situation is that the problem is Sam's, not mine. The second way of looking at the situation is that I think Sam doesn't like me. I may be wrong, but even if I am right, it's still Sam's problem. There may or may not be something I can do to help Sam; however, unless he comes to me with this problem, there is very little I can do to be of assistance.

Yet fear tells me I need to fix something that I can't fix. In some cases, where I am aware of the issue, I may choose to change for Sam's benefit. In other cases I may choose not to. Either way, it's still up to Sam to handle his end of the bargain, just as it's up to me to handle my end when I have a problem with Sam. The point is that I need to take care of me and let Sam take care of Sam, and I need to let go of the fear around the issue; I can't be everybody's friend anyway.

By taking a careful look at how I think about things, I can change my level of fear right off the bat. I can usually downgrade my fear by changing the way I see things or by asking a couple of discerning questions of myself, such as: "Is this something real, or is it something I think is real?" or "Is this really my problem, my issue, or should I let the other person own it?" By taking ownership of what's mine and allowing other people to do the same, I can overcome a lot of my fears before they get a chance to overwhelm me. I can begin to look at things more clearly and learn to identify what I need to change about myself.

As I've learned to apply this practice of assigning ownership, I've found that my self-esteem has grown. I no longer worry so much about what other people think of me because most of it isn't real anyway; it's only what I think they think. On the other hand, if someone wants to tell me what he or she thinks of me and I consider it to be negative, then I can accept it without taking it personally. I can allow this person to have his or her opinion, and I can have mine. Sometimes, because I have learned to remain calm about their opinion of me, we can have a conversation and reveal our disagreements. Then we can make a more informed choice about how important it is to maintain the relationship. I can do so without all the anxiety I used to have regarding things like this. In order to do so, though, I need to make conscious decisions. I can't just react to life, or to fear; I have to think about what's going on in my own head. In working through this process I have come to see life as a series of individual choices and consequences, and this has helped me to deal with my fear as well. I used to be afraid to conquer my fear because I thought I would lose the excuses I had for all my future mistakes. After all, if I am afraid to do something, I have an excuse not to try it; if I do try it, I have an excuse for failing. I can blame failure on my fear, even if I only do this in the privacy of my own head. I've come to see this way of thinking as reactionary living, and I choose to live a proactive life now. Reaction results in distraction. I want a life where I take action based upon my own thoughts and ideas of how things should be. Since I changed the way I look at how life works, I've changed how I see fear.

When I began making my change from reactive to proactive living—from letting life happen to me to making my life happen—I began to see a shift in my thinking. I began to see my life as a series of choices and consequences. I make choices, and those choices bring me consequences. This is true whether I'm living reactively or proactively, since even if I choose not to choose (if I choose to let life happen to me), I have still made a choice. This choice, whatever it is or was, will bring me consequences. Usually, such consequences will be of the sort I see as bad or undesirable, because I didn't take any action in the matter. This is fertile ground for fear.

I made the choice to revamp the helpline. The consequences of that choice were mostly positive. There is now an all-volunteer staff with experience in recovery answering the phones. When people call in for help, they get someone trained to help instead of a paid answering service whose employees have no idea what the organization does to help people. There are now nearly one hundred volunteers answering the phones, and their doing so provides them the opportunity to be of service to their community and to be allowed a chance to feel good about themselves for "doing their part" in the process.

The truth is that I have a hard time finding any negative consequences regarding my choice to revamp the helpline. If I stretch my imagination to find a negative consequence, it might be that I had to work many shifts until the volunteers began to trickle in; but even that was a good thing because the way I see it, I received the chance to meet new people, make new friends, and help others in the process.

If I had failed in this mission, things would have remained the same for the most part, as the helpline would have continued to employ the paid answering service. Yet, if I looked hard enough, I could have found some positive consequences in my failure. I would have learned what not to do when setting up a helpline, and I could have tried again, using my new knowledge as a guide. Even bad or undesirable consequences can be good. Therefore, I no longer fear consequences. I see them as a direct result of my choices, and probably the most amazing thing I've learned about this process is that consequences lead to more choices. Some say that success begets success and, thankfully, failures eventually beget success, although it may not seem like it at the time.

Success resembles a closed loop, or a merry-go-round. I make a choice, there are consequences, and consequences provide more choices. Since fear likes to ride on this merry-go-round, it too is part of the process. It rides along patiently and tells me I need to worry about the next set of consequences I will encounter.

Sometimes I make good choices, and sometimes bad, yet I can easily assign "good" and "bad" labels based on what I think is desirable or undesirable. Sometimes I don't really know if I made a good choice until I see the consequences of that choice. Then I attach my labels. As long as I made the choice and did my best to do things right, I can't find fault in myself for trying—or at least I shouldn't. After all, at the very least I've created a learning opportunity. Failure is an opportunity to learn.

If I make a choice and follow it through to its logical conclusion, I will discover my consequences, which I will certainly label as either good or bad, success or failure. Today in my world, both labels are good, but it wasn't always that way. With success, I am happy because things went according to plan; people are happy. With failure, I may be humiliated, even ridiculed, but I'll have another opportunity to learn, and learning is what makes life worth living. This is why I need to make my decisions very consciously and conscientiously, paying strict attention to how and why I've come to the decision. After all, my decisions, and the actions I take on them, will determine my consequences.

I don't see myself (or anyone else) getting off the merry-go-round of choices and consequences anytime soon, so I've come to believe it's important to participate in my choices—to choose to choose. Then I do my best to learn from the consequences that follow, be they positive or negative, good or bad, success or failure. I do my best not to let fear of those potential consequences stop me from doing what I need to do.

## Realizing That Fear Really Only Takes Two Forms

The best way I know to overcome fear is by experience. When I face something frightening, I must face it head-on and walk through the fear, doing the next right thing the best I can. When I do this, fear shrinks. *When I shrink away from fear, it grows in every corner of my life.* Only fear or courage can dominate. Only one can take the lead, so my choice is simple: I can feed my fear or I can feed my courage. It's like the old story about the two dogs, one scary and the other rather likable. A version goes like this:

A man said, "Inside me there are two dogs. One dog is evil and the other is good. They fight all the time." When asked which dog wins, he reflects for a moment and replies, "The one I feed the most."

I see fear and courage in the same way. The one that wins is the one I feed the most. If I feed the fear, fear wins, and I end up angry or depressed because anger is fear projected and depression is fear internalized.

I came to this conclusion after taking yet another look at how fear works in my life. This time I came to see only two sources of fear. Either I am afraid I will lose something I want to keep, or I'm scared I won't get something I want. When I looked at fear in this way, I was able to see just how small fear really is—and how selfish I can be when I act in fear. It's pretty selfish to fear not getting something, no matter how badly I may want it, and it's rather petty to fear losing something I already have. Sure, there are some justifiable fears. For example, I worry about someone breaking into my house and stealing my stuff. I also have great concerns about keeping my job so I can maintain my current lifestyle. But if I look at these things rationally, I come to see that burglars have rarely stolen from me, and the things they have stolen have been replaced. I also see that while I have lost jobs in the past, I've always managed to find another one. I'm not usually dealing with material things when it comes to getting what I want or losing something I have. Most of the time I fear losing face or not being recognized, and these are irrational fears. They are fears of what other people might think of me.

Because fear likes to look all dressed up and complicated, it can be difficult to see a particular instance of fear as fitting into either the "what am I afraid of losing," or "what am I afraid I won't get," categories, but if I look hard enough, I can usually do it. Often it takes time to figure out what I will lose or not gain in a given situation. This is particularly true when the thing to be lost or not gained is emotional or spiritual rather than material. It is simply hard to measure or calculate. At these times I need to rely on faith—I need to trust the process, knowing fear will be a part of it—and just do the next right thing. It may not be until I look back that I can see what I stood to gain or lose. Only then can I know what I have discovered about myself. What have I given up because of the action? If I lose something, the thing I feared losing is just what I needed to get rid of in order to move on with my life.

As I began to see fear as losing something I want to keep or not getting something I want, I began to see fear like a ghost. I'm a fan of ghost stories, and in ghost stories the ghost itself can't harm anyone without his or her help. A ghost can't cause physical harm; it can only scare someone into doing something where the action taken causes the harm. In ghost stories, the ghost usually scares the person into doing something like jumping out of a window. The ghost didn't do anything to cause the person physical harm. It only raised enough fear to cause the person to harm himself.

When I address fear in this manner, I can see it for what it is. It's just a big boogeyman that likes to make me do things I wouldn't do if the fear wasn't there to influence me. In order to overcome my fear, I must look the ghost in the eye and say, "You aren't going to influence my decisions. I know what I need to do, and I intend to do it. You might as well go bother someone else."

The more I do this, the more I feed my courage, and the more I feed my courage, the more it grows. By my walking through my fear, less energy is available for the fear in my life. My fear will eventually starve. When fear discovers there is nothing for it to gain at my house, it will move on and search out other sources of energy.

Fear has limitations. When I calmly and rationally identify these limitations, I not only see fear for what it really is, I can learn to overcome it. This isn't to say that fear will leave me completely, or forever. I'm not so naive as to believe that, but I have learned that I can reduce fear to a point where nearly all the fear I have is constructive. This is where fear becomes a tool I can use.

## Fear Is Just Part of the Process

Constructive fear is the fear that sets butterflies free in my stomach before I give a speech or puts me on the edge of my seat before a job interview. These kinds of fear help me perform by pushing me to do my best. They are still fears that fall into the above-mentioned categories, fear of failure and fear of not getting something I want. Yet I can use them to my advantage. It takes patience and practice to make it work for me, but I have found it to be a wonderful use of fear. I know it's part of the process of giving a speech or interviewing for a job, so I can put it to good use.

When I say fear is just part of the process, I don't mean to minimize it by using the word just. My intention is to put fear in its place. When used properly, fear is a tool. And everything is a process. Life is a process—we are born, we live, we die. That's an oversimplification, of course, but it contains a grain of truth. We have no control over being born, and we have little or no control over when and how we die, unless it's by suicide. We do have some control over how we live, and life itself is nothing more than a series of processes, choices, and consequences.

I owe this lesson to one of my first writing professors. She told me that I needed to learn to enjoy the process of writing. I have. While learning to write, which is a much larger process than I ever could have imagined, I learned that every action, every step, can be broken down into smaller processes. There are steps taken to accomplish any task. If I follow the steps laid out on the cake mix box, I'll end up with a cake. If I want to become an electrician, there is a process I must go through. Everything in life is like this. It's only a matter of finding, then following, the correct process in order to reach a specific goal. Fear is part of nearly every process, yet when I learn to see fear for what it is, I can overcome it and reach my goal. Most processes can be broken down into even smaller processes, which is a great way to manage things that only seem overwhelming when looked at in a larger context. Since fear usually makes things look overwhelming, I break down each process into smaller processes. When I do, I break down fear too.

I remember going back to school at the age of forty-five and thinking how scared I was of what might or might not happen. My fear ran amok. I asked myself, "Will I be accepted? Can I handle the classes, or am I too old to learn? Will my grades be good enough? How will I pay for everything?" My fear-generated list was nearly endless, so I broke it down. First, I decided to enroll. Then I took one class. That went well enough, so the following semester I took two classes. Soon I was a full-time student carrying a 4.0 grade point average. Eventually, I graduated with honors. It was a process, daunting when I looked at it in one big chunk, yet manageable when I broke it into smaller pieces. I actually broke each semester into weeks, because I found that at the beginning of each semester when I got a syllabus for every class, the amount of work seemed overwhelming. Fear appeared like a ghost and told me I would never get it all done. As I broke things down into weeks, I saw that I could easily do what needed to be done a week at a time. I eventually broke things down into a daily schedule, which made my workload even more manageable. The fear, which started out looking like Frankenstein's monster, began to look more like a simple household chore when I began breaking it down into smaller tasks. The work of going back to school finally became enjoyable as I integrated it into my daily routine. I made learning a process—a set of steps to follow in order to achieve a goal—and it worked out very well. Since then I have found that everything is a process. Everything can be broken down into manageable chunks. Learning to do even this was a process; it wasn't easy, but it is possible.

It took patience and practice, but life is like that. What I practice today, I become better at tomorrow. My goal now is to make every day a practice session for the future. I practice learning so it will become habit. I practice overcoming fear for the same reason. Habits are easy to follow, and dealing with fear can become a habit if I practice it often and if I break it down into a process. It too can be done, and more easily than I ever imagined.

Here are the steps I take nowadays to deal with fear: first, I recognize the fear at a conscious level; I acknowledge it and even mentally shake hands with it. Then I look fear in the eye and tell it I will not let it govern my life, that I plan to do exactly what needs to be done to attain my goal. Then I break the task down into smaller and smaller pieces, breaking fear down as I go, until I discover that the task is not only doable, but also enjoyable. When I reach this point, I almost always find that fear has left the building or is cowering in the corner.

Then I remind myself that fear will return, and I will need to deal with it again, because fear is like that—it's just part of the process.

I have come to believe that fear only exists to be conquered. Sure, I know the fight-or-flight response to fear, the gut reaction to that nagging feeling that something isn't quite right, that something is terribly wrong, or that I'm in a dangerous situation. By conquering fear I mean not simply taking the gut feeling and running with it. What I mean is taking the time to stand up to fear and thinking it through before I act. Often this means stopping and taking time to think, feel, and get to know myself in order to recognize that I am afraid. Then I take time to stop again to give myself an opportunity to think *before* I act.

Sometimes it is prudent to run. If my life is in immediate danger, running is the most likely option. Since that is rarely the case, I have found that more often it is better to stand and face my fears, to think things through, and then do what I decide is the right thing to do, no matter what fear tells me I should do. It may be the more difficult thing to do, but it gets easier every time I do it. Practice makes progress.

I have a fear of heights. My sister asked me if I wanted to go skydiving. My first reaction was "Are you crazy?" But after I thought about it, I went. We did a tandem jump where I was securely attached to a skilled skydiver, who had made thousands of jumps and wore a parachute attached to his back. It was hard to jump from an airplane 13,000 feet in the air, but I did it. And you know what? I still have my fear of heights. When I stand at the edge of a ten-story building, my gut still jumps into my throat. It doesn't bother me as much as it used to. One skydiving attempt did not remove my fear of heights. It only shrank it a little.

I am sure it would subside with more work, but I have made a choice. I have decided, at least for the time being, that I will not be doing more work on this particular fear. Jumping out of airplanes isn't something I care to do again anytime soon. But I'm not ruling it out, either. My sister loves it. She even got my mother to jump—it was my sister's second jump—and she asked me to go again. I declined. But I didn't decline due to fear. I declined because I had something else I wanted to spend my money on at the time.

The next time my sister asks me, I may just go. I know it would be fun. It was fun the first time I jumped, and I know it will help me deal with my fear of heights. In the meantime, I'll keep working on things a bit closer to the ground.

## 02 | Anger and Depression

In my experience, anger and depression are two insidious ways the cunning entity known as fear disguises itself, and as we know, disguises are often intended to conceal the identity of someone or something that wishes us no good.

But anger and depression are two feelings I can easily recognize if I am paying attention. Therefore, I do my best to watch for these two emotions, and when they begin to rear their ugly heads, I look for the fear behind them. Sometimes it is easy to identify the source; other times the fear is more elusive. Yet I can always hunt it down if I am diligent in my quest.

Sometimes I must get more honest with myself than I would like. I must face some facts about myself that I don't want to face, and admit that I am afraid of something I would not like to admit—even to myself. But it helps me locate the core of the problem, which helps me find a solution. Today I'm all about solutions, so I'm willing to make the admission, at least to myself. After all, I want life to be enjoyable. I despise being angry, and I dislike feeling depressed. Therefore, I have spent a lot of time looking for ways to defeat these two thieves of my time and life-energy.

## Depression

When my first sponsor died in 2006, I fell into a mild depression. I call it mild because it seemed moderate for losing someone who had been such a tremendous help to me during my early years of recovery, someone with whom I had become so close. Someone I loved. As it turns out, it was a rather mild case, too. I cried only once. As I look back on this time, I can see that my grieving was reduced by the fact that he was old and his death was imminent. However, the greatest contributor to the mildness of my depression was the fact that we had a wonderful relationship. We never argued, we did many things together, he taught me a lot about staying in recovery and about life itself, and I truly loved him.

While death is a permanent loss, I knew he would live on with me, in my heart. Still, there was depression, albeit mild considering the occasion. I stopped to look at the reason for the depression. This was a case where it was easy to identify the cause. I had lost a great friend, but it didn't stop there. The fear ran through me because I was uncertain of how life would go on without my sponsor. Whom would I turn to when I needed to talk? Who would provide me the advice and love that I got from him for five years? I had doubts about the future, and fear took advantage of this by slithering into my being and rocking my foundation. I had another sponsor lined up, but the fear of losing something I didn't want to lose rode me hard, and the fear of not getting what I thought I might need in the future cracked the whip to egg my fear on.

I was amazed at what happened next. The grieving process was short and disturbed my life very little, even though I was distressed over the loss of a loved one—the one closest to me outside my immediate family. However, I had identified my fear, and I had discovered that I really only had to grieve for my loss and my fear of filling his shoes because of the wonderful relationship we had over the years.

While it may sound as though I am making this process of grieving rather simple, it was even simpler than I expected, and fear took advantage of that, too. For a time I was concerned that I wasn't grieving properly. I thought that maybe I had lost my ability to grieve properly or that I was growing cold-hearted. My sponsor was my first close personal loss since entering recovery, so this was new turf for me. Then I got an email from a friend whom my sponsor had also sponsored. She wrote:

> Mark,
>
> How are you doing? Several times, I think, I am going to pick up the phone and call Chauncey, then I remember, damn, I can't. I know he is with me and my spirit can call him, but have you felt that way? I know he wanted to go [he was in a lot of pain] and I was happy for him. I also know he didn't want to leave his wife Viv, but he has been ready for some time now. How lucky we were to have worked with the best. 1941 [the year he got clean], wow! I feel extremely blessed to have had him in my life. He came at a very crucial time. I will miss him.

This helped me to feel a little better, but it also got me thinking. This is when I truly discovered the how and why of the ease of my transition through my depression over losing a loved one. I learned even more than that, though, and I will discuss that in a moment, but first let me show you how I responded. I wrote:

I am doing very well. For a while, I was getting a little out of sorts around 9:00 every night because that was when I called him. I have overcome that with the knowledge that I can talk to him anytime now—just like I talk to God—and I call Vivian every night.

I have responded overly well to his passing, and I was even worried about how easily I have taken this whole thing, but I think it has a lot to do with the fact that I have no regrets about my relationship with him. I got to do a ton of stuff with him; I talked to him every day for over four years—more often than I talk to my own family members—and I shared my life with him. And now I do the best I can to honor him by living up to the things he taught me.

We were truly blessed by his presence in our lives. There is no doubt about that, and now it is our turn to bless others. He loved to say, "I got mine, you get yours," and there are many ways that can be taken. Today I take it to mean that he had his journey, and now it is up to me to enjoy mine. In fact, I believe that if I don't enjoy my life I am wasting my time.

I miss Chauncey on occasion, but I don't spend a lot of time dwelling on that in a negative manner. Instead I do my best to remember to do what he would have me do, and it isn't very hard to know what he would advise in most situations—the next right thing. As long as I keep it simple and keep my hand out to help the next person, I am carrying the message. And that is what Chauncey would have me do—carry the message!

Love,
Mark

While writing this email, I learned some very important things about grieving, especially when it comes to losing a loved one. I can lessen the depression by living well and maintaining my relationships while my loved ones are still alive. I have discovered that much of my grief and depression when someone close to me dies comes not from my sense of loss, but from my guilt over the things I wished I had done differently—my regrets—and the fear that builds in me from the fact that I will no longer have the opportunity to make things right.

I never had to make things right with Chauncey because we got off to a good start. We kept our relationship in proper working order throughout the remainder of his life. I have had to do some work on other relationships, which I neglected for a long time while I was drinking and drugging, and that is putting it very kindly. Today I do my best, on a daily basis, to live a good life and carefully maintain relationships with those I love.

I have taken the long way around the block to learn this important lesson, but I think there was good reason to take that little detour. I hope this little side trip will encourage us all to put more effort into the relationships that mean the most to us. Identifying fear in the midst of depression can be the last thing I want to do; however, if I can dredge up the will to look at the real cause of depression—fear—I can usually take the necessary steps to relieve its severity. In fact, quite often, simply taking some action in an attempt to come out of the depression will help me feel better. Many times doing something is better than doing nothing, but other times there is another solution.

## Enjoying Depression

"Enjoying" depression may sound a little crazy, but it works for me every time. Of course, I'm not talking about clinical depression or anything that might require a doctor's help or medication; I'm talking about regular, run-of-the-mill depression—what the experts call "dysthymia." I discovered that enjoying my depression worked for me after talking with my sponsor.

One night when I called Chauncey, I was in a foul mood; I was depressed after having a bad day and didn't know what to do to feel better. I can't recall the exact reason for my mood, but I know it was real, and I know I was quite sad. After our usual cordial greeting, I started to talk about my bad day. I told him about my issues and said I was depressed. He replied, "Well, enjoy that."

I said, "Enjoy it? What are you, nuts? I'm feeling depressed. How can I enjoy that?"

His reply was simple and direct, as usual. He told me that I should always enjoy my state of mind and my emotions. "They won't kill you," he said, "so why not learn to relax into them instead of fighting them?"

As usual, I was stumped at first, but after thinking about it I decided to try it. I figured that as long as I was going to be depressed, I might as well go ahead and enjoy the feeling, or at least go ahead and feel it, instead of fighting it. It took some serious conscious effort, but I made up my mind to do the best I could to relax into the depression and feel it, even though I didn't think it would do me much good.

A surprising thing happened once I truly allowed myself to relax into the depression instead of spending most of my energy trying to fight it. While I actually felt slightly more depressed or felt it more intensely for a short time, I discovered that I had actually made a choice in the matter.

Instead of fighting a losing battle and continuing to feel bad, I chose to fully embrace the mood and let it have its way. I discovered that since I chose to feel bad, I could just as easily choose to feel good, although at first I wasn't sure it would work.

For a short time, I reveled in my bad mood. At first I didn't seem to have enough desire to change. However, after feeling depressed—especially feeling it with the intensity I was feeling it with after allowing it to have its way—I decided that I needed to do something about it. I decided I wanted to feel happy, or at least not quite as sad. And since simply fighting the depression had never worked before, I figured I would try being happy instead. What happened next was amazing.

I decided to be happy. Of course, it didn't happen quickly; it took a little while, but I changed my mood faster than I ever had before. I changed it by changing it, not by fighting it. I learned to substitute happiness for sadness. It was like changing the station on the radio or choosing a different item from the menu at a restaurant, only not so fast.

You see, prior to this, I had always said to myself, "I will not be sad, I will not be sad," or "I am sick of feeling depressed; I need to do something." In this way I was maintaining focus on the sadness, and the bad mood survived and thrived, or at least lingered. When I took action toward literally changing my mood by shifting from sadness to happiness, it worked.

The first time I did this it took a while. But the more I have practiced it, the better I am at making the transition. This focus works for any mood. I can change from happy to sad if I want to, although it is harder for me because I always practice going the other way. I still can't seem to make a case for wanting to trade a good mood for a bad one.

Since I needed to figure out ways to make myself happy, I had to do some homework. Through doing my homework, I have discovered several ways to change my mood, two of which are my favorites.

The first way to change my mood is through helping someone else. It doesn't matter how I help them; it only matters that I do something for someone besides myself. I can hold a door open. Although that is a small thing, it does help me feel better, and I might have to do it many times before I make real progress. I have taken to shoveling snow for my elderly neighbors because wintertime in Michigan is a dull, boring, and depressing time of year, and because helping others helps ward off depression. The bigger the act of helping, the quicker I change my mood. Because helping others improves my mood, I usually look for opportunities in the course of an ordinary day. In this way, I work to maintain my good mood on a consistent basis, and at the same time I look for ways to help others, should I fall into a bad mood.

The other way I have found to change my mood comes from a saying I heard. Maybe I read it in a fortune cookie, but I don't actually remember for sure. It says, "You can't make someone else laugh without laughing yourself."

While this can be more difficult than actually doing nice things for other people—because it is hard to find funny things to say or do when I feel down—it does work. And since just thinking of funny things can make me laugh, I can do this without anyone else around. I can read a funny book if my thinker seems mired in depression. I have purchased a few good joke books for just such occasions, and I am always on the lookout for good, funny books to put in my library for use during these times.

My sponsor taught me that problems were opportunities. For some people, changing their mood is a problem. I see a mood change as an opportunity to grow. The important thing to remember is that I work to change the mood, not fight against it, trying to make it go away. I need to provide a substitute—a better mood—just like when I replace bad habits with good ones. *I should change my mood after I allow myself to feel the bad mood for a short time.* By allowing myself to feel the undesirable mood, it helps create a quicker, more stable transition. It also helps me realize that a bad mood won't hurt me and provides me with proof that I can choose my moods more easily than I might think.

When I fight against something, I have to keep it around. I can't fight with another person if they leave my location, and I can't fight a bad mood if it goes away, either. I believe that is why a bad mood sticks around if I fight it—because I need it for there to be a fight. For it to fight me, I must breathe life into it and prop it up. Without me, my bad mood cannot get bigger or stronger. Once I surrender to the mood and let it have its way for a time, the fight ends and I can dismiss it; I can let it go. If I don't enjoy feeling poorly, then why not let it go? I have found that the easiest way to let one thing go is to replace it with something else, something I enjoy, like a good mood.

Dealing with simple depression is easier than I used to think. With a little practice I can make the switch from depressed to happy in a much shorter time than I ever could before, by using a couple of simple little tricks. I can also keep depression and other bad moods at bay by practicing these tricks on a daily basis. To do so, I need to do a little extra work each day, such as holding doors for others and being nice to people I don't even know. I find that it is well worth the effort. Because of my many options, I find that there are several things that I can do to maintain my good mood.

One important tool I use is watching what I think. I will examine this more a little later. For now, let's move on to anger—fear turned outward.

## Anger

I don't get mad very often, and there is good reason for that: it doesn't do anything positive for me. Confucius said, "When anger rises, think of the consequences." Unfortunately for me, once anger rises I do not think very well, let alone think of possible consequences. Therefore, I have found it best to notice anger at its first signs and stop it in its tracks by thinking of potential consequences as well as alternative courses of action. It is at this critical moment that I need not only to consider Confucius's words of wisdom, but also another quotation from ancient times, by Pubilius Syrius, "You can accomplish by kindness what you cannot by force." If the kind thing to do is to bite my tongue, this is the time to do it. I can usually apply a little restraint early in the process (and avoid biting my tongue off altogether), or I can let it run rampant later and suffer the consequences.

Anger is easy to recognize if I know what to look for. We all know what it feels like physically when anger begins to grow within us. And while we usually do not make a conscious list of the physical effects—the elevated blood pressure, the increased heart rate, the knot in our stomach—we can usually identify these manifestations as anger when they occur.

I do my best these days to be on the lookout for anger for two main reasons. First, I want to know that I am dealing with rising anger as early as possible. Second, I want to slow or stop its progress before it overtakes my mental capacity and reduces or eliminates my ability to deal with it in a productive manner.

The main reason I want to identify my anger before it takes over is that I have learned something important about anger, something I discovered during my recovery that I never considered until it confronted me through other people in the program. You see, I used to believe that someone or something had made me mad. Today I know better.

You cannot make me mad. No one can make me mad. Nothing can make me mad.

While anger is often considered a part of the human fight-or-flight response to a perceived threat, whether real or imagined, it can quickly take over my entire being if I do not take conscious control of my situation. Allowing anger to run my life—even for a short time—can cause me to do things I will later regret. I believe this happens when I am angry or stressed beyond any reasonable or normal measure. If I can't think straight due to stress, then I am not really my normal, calm self, and I am liable to say and do things that I would not do if I were in a calm, relaxed state.

Therefore, I find it best to see the anger coming and either lock the door and deny it entry, or open the front and back doors, allowing it to pass through quickly—hopefully without making much of a mess. After all, if I allow anger to run me for very long, and I do things I will regret, others affected by my anger will not soon forget my outburst. Nor will they likely allow me to use my anger as an excuse or alibi for my behavior. The potentially more serious issue is that I'm not likely to forgive myself and allow my anger to be an acceptable excuse. There is good reason for this.

You cannot make me mad. No one can make me mad. Nothing can make me mad.

Anger is a choice. For anger to control and dominate me, I must allow it. Anger cannot make me do anything unless I let it. People can do things that I don't like. They can even do things to me that I don't like. But I still have to choose, consciously or not, to be angry about it, or at the very least I must know that it is I who allow anger to take over my situation.

When I was introduced to the idea that anger was a choice, I rejected it. After all, I was used to saying things like "You made me mad," which put the blame on the other person, or so I thought.

The truth is that you did something, I didn't like it, and I got angry!

My choice of words, my saying to you, "You made me mad," made it seem as though it was your fault that I got mad. I have discovered through trial and error that I can choose not to get mad almost anytime I want.

There are exceptions to every rule, and no matter how hard I try I will still get angry, but that doesn't mean I should not take responsibility for my anger. It is my emotion—not yours. Since it is my emotion, if I say, "You made me mad," then you made me mad because I let you, I gave you permission, and I gave you control of my emotions—even if subconsciously, and only for a moment, I handed over control of my being to you. Whomever or whatever it is that I allowed to make me mad, I still gave control of myself over to someone or something outside myself.

Knowing and understanding this about me, I take close control of my anger whenever I catch it rearing its ugly head. I also take control of it because anger is a tool. Used properly, my anger has benefits, but only if I choose to see it that way.

Anger tells me that something is wrong. Sometimes there is something wrong with the way other people are acting or the things they are doing. Other times I may get angry at the state of the world and the way those in control are running things. There are too many things to get mad about to list them all here. But as I have watched my anger, I have noticed that no matter where the anger comes from, no matter the cause, anger is telling me that something is wrong.

The truth is: whatever is wrong is usually wrong with me.

Of course, there are times when I can justifiably and properly carry my anger. I imagine I would be angry if someone robbed me or held me up at gunpoint. But the more likely reasons for my anger stem from everyday occurrences such as someone pulling out in front of me in traffic, a coworker causing problems at work, or someone trying to cut in front of me in line at the supermarket. When one of these things happens, anger can grow quickly, and I am liable to act out unless I can catch the anger and channel its energy into something more productive.

What can be more productive is a solution. If someone pulls out in front of me, the solution can be as simple as allowing them to go about their business while letting go of any anger attached to the situation. Odds are that in an hour or two I will have forgotten about the situation anyway. A potentially more serious situation can come from a coworker who has caused a problem at work. Maybe they have taken credit for my work and I think I need that credit in order to secure a promotion; this is the fear of not getting something I want. Odds are that getting angry will not make matters lean more in my favor. The boss is not likely to believe me, let alone give me credit, if I begin to rant and rave during our meeting that so-and-so "stole" my idea. Such a response sounds rather childish and will not curry any favor with my boss.

If I allow my anger to control my situation, I am apt to do just that—rant and rave. However, if I can get a grip on my anger, I can handle myself more appropriately in the situation. I can keep my cool and my ability to think, and I can address the issue with a calm resolve to correct the misunderstanding.

There is an old saying: "He who strikes the first blow admits he's lost the argument." If I strike the first blow in a meeting, whether the blow is physical or verbal, I may lose my opportunity to take corrective action, and may appear rather juvenile in the process. My anger, which has signaled to me that something is wrong, can actually come in handy by giving me the necessary resolve to correct the issue. But I may ruin any future attempt at corrective action if I blow up in front of a roomful of my coworkers. I need to remember that just because my sneaky coworker has claimed responsibility for my great idea, it doesn't mean that is the last word on the subject.

Things can often be corrected or fixed.

I remember leaving a meeting to go to lunch with a young man I was sponsoring. We were in my car and had gone only a few blocks when we stopped at a red light to wait for it to turn green. While we were sitting still, another car hit us. The accident was by no stretch of the imagination my fault; my car wasn't even moving when we were hit.

I got out of my car to see if the people in the other car were okay, even though I was certain they were because the accident took place at less than ten miles per hour. When the occupants of the other vehicle and I met for the first time, we began discussing how to handle the situation. They were on their lunch hour and needed to get back to work; we were on our way to lunch and were hungry. Neither car was damaged badly, but both cars would spend some time in the repair shop.

The person driving the other car said she had never done anything like this before and asked me what we should do. I told her that since she was in a hurry, I thought we could simply exchange information—driver's license, insurance, and phone numbers—and report it to the police at our earliest convenience. She said she would call them when she got back to work. I told her that would be fine, and we went on our way.

When we got back in my car, my sponsee said, "I can't believe the way you handled that." When I asked him if I had done something wrong, he replied, "No, I mean you didn't even get mad. She wrecked your car. Aren't you upset?"

"Of course I'm upset," I replied, "but no one was hurt and cars can be fixed."

"I thought you'd rip that lady a new one," my sponsee said, then laughed and added, "I would have. I know it."

"I think she felt bad enough without getting chewed out," I said. "Still hungry?" Soon we went off to lunch, my sponsee still marveling at my calmness; I was, too, just a little bit. That was the first accident I had been in while in recovery, and I was a little surprised at how calmly I had handled the situation. Then I realized something else.

Until that moment, I had no idea that during the episode my sponsee was eying every move I made. I never did get mad. Sure, I felt anger—based on a fear of losing something I had—but I quickly asked myself what good it would do to let anger run the situation. I decided that anger over the possibility that I would temporarily lose my car would only make things worse, so I dismissed it for cause. Instead, the transaction took place in a calm and orderly fashion. The accident was obviously the other person's fault, and I felt certain the damage on the vehicles would bear that out even if she didn't admit fault. As it happened, after lunch, almost as soon as I got home, there was a knock at my door. A police officer had come to investigate the accident. I showed the officer my car and he said it looked exactly like what he was told. As it turned out, the other driver admitted fault and the rest of the matter was easily resolved. I drove a rental car for a few days while my car was repaired. Things could have happened differently, but I am inclined to believe that the woman acted the way she did because I acted in a civil manner. Had I acted out of anger, it could only have made things worse, because this situation went about as well as an accident can go.

I'm not saying everything in life goes better without anger, or that I can avoid or dismiss anger easily. When this accident happened, I had been practicing dismissing my anger when I felt it would make things worse for some time. On this occasion, I happened to get it right and things went smooth as silk. Life isn't always this simple, but I have experienced enough anger-provoking situations now to realize that remaining calm is the way to go. I can save face by not acting like a crazed person. When I remain calm and keep my wits about me, I can analyze the situation more clearly, be more honest with myself, and generally get better results all around.

## I Get Maddest When I Am Wrong

I hate to admit when I am wrong. I think everybody hates to admit when he or she is wrong. I might be wrong now. Because I hate to admit when I am wrong, I tend to get my defenses up when I find myself in a situation where I know I am at fault. This usually causes me to get angry—angrier than I would be if I knew I was right. Here are two examples, one when I knew I was right and the other when I knew I was wrong. The outcomes were very different.

A good friend once confronted me about how I had handled a situation with the volunteer helpline I was managing. The friend confronted me about a woman who had neglected to show up for a shift. The woman was young and attractive and my friend knew I favored her. She was far too young for me to date, but I liked her just the same. My friend accused me of giving her preferential treatment because of my feelings for her. I disagreed. An argument ensued, albeit one that started out calmly enough. My friend stuck to his guns and I stuck to mine. To prove my point, I suggested that he look at how smoothly things had run during my tenure as manager of the helpline. I calmly explained that when the young woman did not show up, the person on the previous shift called me looking for help. I got in my car, drove in, and took the shift.

My friend claimed that I wouldn't have done that for another person. I pointed out that I did it whenever that sort of thing happened. My friend got mad and refused to believe me. He claimed again and again that I went out of my way to keep the young woman from looking bad. I informed him that since it was a volunteer helpline, there was no one to look bad to besides me, since I was the chairperson. I wasn't bothered by those who did not show up. The helpline was relatively new and people were still not used to the idea that they needed to make sure they covered their shift no matter what else might be happening in their lives. I did my best to make sure every shift operator handled things properly, and when someone didn't show up for his or her shift, I would go in to cover the shift, then have a talk with the person who had failed to work their shift in order to avoid it happening again.

When one of the volunteers did not report for a shift, the volunteer on the previous shift called me looking for relief, and I always followed up with the person who'd missed his or her shift. My game plan was the same for this young woman as it was for the other volunteers. No matter how much I either liked or disliked someone, I had to treat everyone the same. I told this to my friend. He refused to believe me, and his anger grew. Soon he was yelling at me. I sat back in my chair and let him rant. My only response was to remain calm and to reiterate the facts, as I understood them. I did my best to assure him that I would handle the situation as I always did. Finally my friend got up, told me I was hard-headed, and went into the other room.

I felt my own anger rise up, but knowing it would make things worse, I dismissed it and said, as calmly as I could, "I know you are mad. When you calm down maybe we can continue this conversation." This was relatively early in my days of anger management, and I was amazed at the fact that I actually did a decent job of dealing with my anger.

After a few moments, my friend came back and sat down. "You're serious," he said. "You really expect me to believe that you handled this situation just as you would with anyone else."

I assured him that I did, and I would continue to handle these situations in the same manner regardless of who was involved. We continued talking and resolved our differences. Our friendship was undamaged. I continued to handle those situations without prejudice until the day I left that position. Today my friend and I laugh about that conflict. We both learned from it. Moreover, when he said he hated being wrong, it reminded me and educated me about how mad I get when I am wrong.

Looking back on that incident, I realized that every time I have been wrong, I have tended to get angrier than when I was right. The car accident was one situation where I did nothing wrong and I found it easy to dismiss any anger. However, when my mind quickly settles on a situation where I am wrong and I know I am wrong, my anger takes over—seemingly without my permission.

My former girlfriend had set up a dinner date with a couple that she knew. She told me about the dinner date and I agreed to go. When the day came for the date, I had other plans. Forgetting about the date, I had agreed to go out with friends of my own—an obvious mistake on my part. Being wrong, and knowing I was wrong, I got angry. After all, I was going to lose a chance to go out with my friends, and I would look bad in the eyes of my friends who would think that my girlfriend ran the show. I felt I had to defend my position.

I threw a fit, which didn't help me defend my position, which was indefensible, and only made things worse. I argued, trying desperately to make my case. I claimed that she never told me about the dinner date with her friends, which was a lie that only compounded the problem. After fighting a losing battle for a while, I walked away in a huff, only to return when I had cooled down enough to swallow my pride and admit I was wrong.

At this point, I not only had to admit that I was wrong about the argument, but I also had to admit that I had lied as well. Through my anger, I had exacerbated the situation. I did so because I did not want to or could not admit that I was wrong. When I calmed down, I was able to admit my fault. Unfortunately, I placed a thunderhead over what could have been a marvelous evening because I couldn't dismiss my anger over my own mistake. Because of this, and other situations like it, I have learned the importance of catching my anger early, especially when I am wrong. I have also learned to admit my mistakes more readily.

While I doubt that containing my anger would have gotten me out of the dinner date on that occasion, there are times when not losing control of my anger can help me get what I want or need.

## When Anger Drives, I Don't Get to Give Directions

When I am angry, I drive people away from my ideas and the things I may need or want. Even if I am right, people tend to resist me when I act out in anger. I have had occasions, as everyone has, where I found things on my credit card bill that I either didn't order or didn't buy, or that I had returned and was not given proper credit for. I have learned the hard way that yelling at someone over the phone while trying to convince him or her to help me straighten out a problem goes completely against my advantage.

I discovered a charge on my charge card one time for nearly five hundred dollars paid to a health spa in North Carolina. Living in Michigan, I had no reason to join a gym in North Carolina, and, feeling a little self-righteous, I called the credit card company. When I got a person on the line, I began telling them in a not-too-friendly way just how stupid I thought they were for allowing the charge to take place. I ended up canceling the card during the fracas. I paid them what I owed them—minus the charge for the gym—and told them to cancel the card. In fact, if I remember right, I told the person on the phone, the first person I talked to about the incident, to cancel the account. I got a new card from a different company, and went about my business. A month or two later I received a letter from the original card company explaining that they found the problem and had corrected it. Someone had punched in my number instead of the actual number. My card was very similar the one that actually made the purchase, or so they said, and I was improperly charged. The credit card company apologized and offered to reopen my account. While I am sure that they did so because they are a business and, as such, are used to dealing with these kinds of things—including irate customers like me—I had already moved on. I declined their offer. I didn't feel good about myself or how I acted.

Since then I have had several opportunities to correct mistakes by credit card companies and others who have wronged me. I do my best not to raise my voice or let anger rule the discussion at hand in these matters. I know that being firm, not angry, and reactive, not overreactive, will get me what I need in almost every case. I calmly explain myself; sometimes I even point out to the person I am talking to that I know they are not personally responsible for the problem, but that I would greatly appreciate a quick resolution. I show them respect for the job they do and understand that they are there to take phone calls from customers. So far, my calm demeanor has worked every time, and I have no reason to believe it won't continue to work in the future.

Instead of allowing my anger to rise up and take over situations that disrupt my life, I use it to create a firm determination to correct the situation or to make it better. I use anger as an ally these days. I keep it on my team, but I remain the head coach. I tell anger what to do and how to help me. I don't let it run rampant or run things helter-skelter.

Since I have started seeing anger as fear turned outward—toward others—I do my best to find the fear, the root of the problem. Sometimes it is easy to spot; other times it isn't. However, it generally boils down to one of the two main causes of fear I have pointed out: losing something I have and not getting something I want. Since I have started looking for these causes, when I feel anger begin to rise, I have noticed that it gives me a moment to pause. I am able to remove my thoughts from the maddening situation long enough to remain calm, or at least I am calmer than I otherwise might be if I did not see fear in a new light.

There is an ancient Chinese proverb: "If you are patient in one moment of anger, you will escape a hundred days of sorrow." Since I know that anger isn't going to leave my life, I know I must learn to control it—to use it to my advantage—instead of letting it run away with my life. Anger is a form of fear, and I am still learning to deal with fear as well as anger. God willing, I will continue to learn until the day I die.

Since learning is such a huge part of life, let's look at learning.

## 03 | The Learning Experience

Living life in the fast lane caused my spirit to dry up and my desire for learning to dry up as well. I will admit that I never had much of a desire for learning when I was growing up, at least not "book learning." I hated school, and barely made it through high school. When I went to college, which was a requirement in my family, it didn't take long to figure out that I would rather get high than highly educated. I left after two terms so that I could get a job and buy the things that would make me happy. I have learned since then that money and material possessions do not make me happy. I have learned that I am happy when I want to be happy. Unfortunately, it took me a long time to learn this lesson, longer than I would have liked.

On occasion, I wish I had life to do over again so that I could do a better job. There are problems with this line of thinking, though, and after plenty of thought and discussion with trusted friends and family, I have learned to do my best to dispense with these thoughts the same way I throw out thoughts of drinking and drugging. They are, after all, nearly as dangerous—they can lead to the more damaging thoughts of drinking, even providing what seems to be a reasonable justification for crawling back into my old ways.

Since the biggest regret I have in life is that I drank and did other drugs for so much of my life, I once had reason to justify maintaining the regret. I have found a way to deal with the regret in order to keep it from bothering me more than occasionally. I have had to learn some truths about rationalization and justification in order to be able to dismiss these crazy thoughts from my mind before they can do more harm than good. Before I get into how I am able to toss aside my regrets over my lost youth, let me explain how I dealt with the regret itself, since it is the reason for the recurring thoughts, which have all but lost their place in my life.

I drank and did drugs for many years, and though I gave up the drugs at about age thirty, I continued to drink until I was forty-three. That is a large chunk of life to give to self-destructive behavior. When I cleaned up my act and looked back over my life, I discovered I could have done a much better job if I had done some things differently. It was easy to think of ways I could be rich by now if I had done this or how I could be happy if I had done that. I didn't like the fact that I had wasted such a large chunk of my time on this planet. I used to listen to my old "stinking thinking," which told me, "What's the use? I might as well finish it off; let's go get drunk."

I talked to my sponsor and decided to try another angle. I prayed about it. I asked God to help me find a way to rid myself of regret over my misspent past. I prayed for quite some time, and finally the answer came. The answer was humbling, but it seemed like a reasonable solution to my problem. The answer was to see my past as a good example of what not to do with your life—and use it to help others not to do what I had done. It seemed like a simple enough answer, but the only way I could see to put my newfound insight into practice was to work with young people in recovery. After all, I had wasted my youth, and if I was going to help other people not do what I did, I needed to reach them before they made the same mistakes I made.

I talked to God and said that I thought the answer to my problem, the answer He had provided me through prayer and meditation, was to help others to avoid the same mistakes I had made. I went on to say, "If this was what He wanted me to do, I would need to work with young people in order to help them stay on the path to recovery." I ended my prayer with a simple request:

"If you want me to use my past as an example for young people, please put young people in my life for me to help."

Since I made my simple request, I have sponsored more than a dozen people. Only two of them have been over the age of thirty. Since every one of them has asked me to sponsor them, I guess I got my answer. I have worked with many more people whom I did not sponsor, and it seems a rather large percentage of them have been younger, too. In addition, the coolest thing for me is that I get to learn in the process.

Sponsorship, just like mentorship, goes both ways. I have been blessed with helping people who also help me, and who are younger than me, young enough to be my children, and they keep me in touch with what the youth of today are up to. Sometimes I have to fight off new technologies because they want me to try things with which I am not comfortable. At other times, I try their suggestions. The best thing is that I find that it is a wonderful way to get rid of the biggest regret of my life. Today I only have to deal with regret the way I deal with thoughts of drinking and drugging. I dismiss them out of hand, and without cause. These thoughts have no business in my head, so when they show up I bounce them out and turn to something else.

While regretting or wanting to relive my past is one way of wasting time, I have learned there is another, more subtle way of wasting my life. When I was new in recovery I found an amazing sponsor—I actually give God the credit for putting him in my life, but that's another story—who had been in recovery for nearly sixty years when I met him. I was amazed by his time in recovery, and I asked him how in the world someone could stay in recovery that long. Being a humble man, he said, "I didn't use and I didn't die. But I did it one day at a time."

I replied that I wished I had sixty years in recovery. I was only forty-three years old at the time. Looking back, this is funny to me. He came back with "Are you willing to be ninety years old in exchange for that?"

That wiped the smile off my face, and set me straight about wishing my life away. I learned to be careful about how quickly I wish my life away. For years my mother had been telling me not to wish my life away when I would say something like "I can't wait until (you can fill in the blank here) this weekend," or "I can't wait until the Fourth of July." Mom always came back with her standard answer: "Don't wish your life away."

I always laughed at her for saying it, but when my sponsor said, "Are you willing to be ninety years old in exchange for that?" it drove home my mother's point. I went to work changing my habits concerning what I wished for or the things I thought I couldn't wait for.

You see, what I wanted was to know everything he knew to have his happiness, serenity, and humility. What I didn't stop to think of is that it took him ninety years to get to where he was at the time. Learning is a process! Moreover, when I connected my mom's saying, "Don't wish your life away," and my sponsor's question, "Are you willing to be ninety years old in exchange for that?" I got much more than the sum of the two parts. Unfortunately, these two parts came many years apart. You will notice the unfortunately at the beginning of the last sentence—old habits die hard—and it took me that long to get the message.

I have found that if I am actually looking for the answer it will come much sooner than expected, and today I look for answers. I look because learning is the blood coursing through the veins of life. I have decided, at least for me, that when you quit learning, you are dead. Your heart may still beat, you may still move through life, but you are much more dead than alive when you stop learning. I only apply this philosophy to myself. To say it properly, I should say, "When I stop learning, I'm dead." Today I not only truly believe that, I hope it is the case. I hope I continue learning right up until the day I die. It would be okay with me for two reasons. First, there is nothing I can do about the day I die, so recognizing it—especially at that late hour on the last day—wouldn't be a problem. Second, it would be fine not to learn anything on my last day on Earth because I wouldn't be using it for long anyway.

Learning is like a jigsaw puzzle: I never know when two or more pieces are going to come together to create a lesson that is much larger than the sum of the parts. Because of this learning process, I do my best to be on the lookout for learning opportunities. I have gone back to school in search of learning. Even though I have attained two college degrees, I am still going to school. When I went back originally, I did it for one reason: I went to learn something. Probably the most important thing I learned is the importance of learning, itself. The degrees mean little compared to the things I have learned.

## Making Adjustments

It took me a long time to learn that life is full of adjustments. I need to practice making adjustments. If I make them as soon as they are needed, I can head off bigger problems down the road.

I ride a bike during the summer months, and I occasionally adjust the chain. If I don't make some adjustments, I usually have problems, so I have learned to check the chain often. I also have to check the tire pressure to make sure it is within proper limits. These are easy adjustments to make, and I make them when necessary to avoid problems.

The funny thing with life is that I often don't know what adjustments need to be made until something goes wrong. Sometimes what goes wrong is a small thing, and I can correct it easily. However, occasionally I experience what I consider a calamity and I think I need to make major life changes to put things back in order. The most amazing discovery for me, when it comes to these calamities, is that they were usually preceded by several much smaller issues that I could have adjusted for but didn't. As I see it, this is what happened with my using.

As I look back over my years of chemical abuse, I can see several occasions where God provided me with potential eye-openers; some were small, some much larger. Some opportunities I didn't recognize for what they were, and others I ignored. Eventually I faced what I consider a life-threatening situation. My using reached a point where I would need to make an almost unthinkable adjustment to my lifestyle. I would have to quit altogether.

Now, I don't want to debate whether I have or had any choice in becoming an addict. To me that is irrelevant at this point. However, if I had decided to heed one or more of the several warnings that showed me I needed to make adjustments to my life, maybe it would have been a little easier for me. While it may appear that I am trying to relive my life, I am not. The consequences I experienced from not heeding the warnings I was given are a lesson in learning for me. The school of hard knocks gave me the best education I could find.

As I look back, I see many opportunities where I could have changed my behavior, made necessary adjustments, and made a better life for myself. Instead of using, I could have changed; when I was arrested for drugs, I could have changed; when my ex-wife told me I drank too much and she wanted me to stop, I could have changed; but by then things were pretty much out of control. While these are the more severe signs that I needed to adjust my life, they are a long way from being the only signals life gave me.

I got a DUI, I almost lost a job I had managed to hang onto for many years, and my wife divorced me. On and on it went until I became willing to make the proper adjustments in my life and finally put a stop to the unfortunate circumstances I kept creating for myself. I was my own worst enemy, but I could not see my self-destruction for what it was—sheer insanity. Maybe I could have changed earlier; maybe I was destined to make all those mistakes. I won't argue that point because it does not get at the real issue, which is this: today I look for places where life is providing me the opportunity to make adjustments in order to live a better life.

I ignored all the signs that drinking was ruining my life, and all the trouble it was causing me, and the warning signs simply grew larger. The problems continued to pile up, grow, and compound, until I could no longer face the prospect of letting them go any longer. I *had* to do something. My fear of stopping finally outweighed my fear of what would happen if I did not. I began making the proper adjustments in order to change my life.

I now use my ability to make adjustments more quickly. I don't wait until things get so bad that I have what seem to be unbearable choices like those that I had when I was using. Today I look for things I need to work on— things I need to adjust in my life—before they get out of control.

Fear is something I can use to help me discover what in my life I need to change. Instead of insisting that life be a certain way—my way—I am beginning to open my heart to what is my true reality. I am starting to understand that life doesn't adjust to me nearly as easily as I can adjust to it. Because of this new perspective, I now look for ways I can or need to adjust to life as it is.

Some of the most obvious ways I can change in order to make life easier for myself can still be difficult. Learning to be patient and tolerant looks like it is going to be a lifelong ordeal, but today that is okay. I look for opportunities to work on these aspects of myself. When I look for them, I find them.

I used to attend a particular meeting a few years ago. A woman consistently came in late. She would show up forty-five minutes into an hour-long meeting. Then, when the meeting was over and everyone had shared, the chairperson would invite her to share. She would go on for a couple of minutes about why she was late before she even got down to the business of sharing. Her tardiness and apparent disregard for others aggravated me to no end. Then I opened my heart to what was happening instead of insisting things be different to suit me. The situation turned out to be an opportunity for me to work on my lack of patience and my intolerance. It wasn't easy, and not just for me, either. I found that the situation bothered other people as well.

Every week this woman repeated her process. Arriving half an hour late was early for her, or so it seemed. She usually ran forty-five minutes late, give or take a few minutes. Every time she walked into the meeting, it grated on my nerves. When she spoke—taking far longer than I figured she should talk—she often kept us past the normal ending time. We often didn't close the meeting until five or ten minutes after the hour because of her blathering. I decided something needed to change. I also knew I was the only one who could make the necessary adjustments. I had to find a different meeting or I had to become more patient and tolerant of this woman.

Finding another meeting was the most appealing option, I'll admit, but I decided to stay put. She wasn't going to change, or so I figured, and that would provide me the opportunity to change myself and to adjust. For several months I endured; each week I felt the tension rise when she walked into the room.

Then, one week, the chairperson asked her if she would like to share. I had not noticed that she was there. I hadn't seen her come in, although I knew she was late because she was not there when the meeting began. It was a relatively small meeting, ten or fifteen people, and I knew everyone who attended. We all said hello before the meeting began, and I was sure she was not there. Yet here she was, popping up on the radar for the first time when the chairperson asked her to speak. Then something truly amazing happened. I discovered I wasn't the only one working on my patience and tolerance. When the woman began to tell why she was late, the woman sitting next to me said, "You're late every week. We don't need an excuse every time." I had to bite my tongue to keep from laughing. After the meeting, I had a talk with the woman who made the comment. We were good friends and could say anything to each other, so I mentioned to her that she could use some work on her patience and tolerance. When she stopped laughing, she agreed. Then she said that everyone could do some work on patience and tolerance. We went on to have a conversation about the lady who came in late, and I told her how I had decided to continue coming to this meeting until I was relieved of my anguish over her tardiness. She asked me if I ever thought that would happen. I told her that I thought it had happened, just that evening. When she asked me how I knew, I told her that I had not noticed when the tardy women came in late that night.

I continued to attend that meeting for a few months to make sure I was completely over the woman's tardiness. Week after week, she still came in late. Either I did not notice when she came in, or when she did, it did not bother me. I knew I had made gains in improving my patience and tolerance. Even though I eventually left that meeting to attend another, I did so not because I was running away from change, but because I was looking for more. My friend told me a few months later that she had also become more patient after she learned what I was doing. She said she took a long look at herself and decided that she was afraid to change, but that she was, quite suddenly, more afraid to avoid that change. Her revelation led me to even more learning opportunities. We never seem to stop to think about the other person's fear. I know it is something that rarely, if ever, crosses my mind. I don't stop to think that other people might have fears as I do or what they might actually be.

As I look back at the lady who was a late arrival to every meeting, I imagine that fear probably played a role, if not in her being late, then certainly in her spending two minutes explaining why she had been late. I am certain that fear drove her to make excuses. What these fears might have been is beyond me, and I refuse to speculate because I am sure I would be wrong, but I am certain that fear played a role. Even if she only gave her excuses in order to allay her fear of others judging her, fear of what others think was probably sitting right there on her shoulder and occupying her mind.

It is easy to look back and see how I might have missed something. It is much more difficult to reach out for help while things are happening and to consider that people I interact with might be afraid of me or of other things, and that this fear might cloud their thoughts and influence their actions. I still have trouble because I see no reason to be afraid of me. I know I am harmless. I am certainly not one to be afraid of, so why should I make someone nervous?

Well, the answer doesn't really matter. I guess I could answer, "Why not?" but that wouldn't help me either. I don't really need to know why someone may be afraid of me in order to work on this area of my life. I only need a little patience and to allow for some mistakes along the way. I will most likely forget to consider that other people have fears, as I do. I may not be very tolerant of people who judge me based on their fears. These are some of the things that I can work on to make myself into a better person. After all, if I want a life full of love, I must be the source of that love; I must become the change I want to see in the world. I must be the source of what I want to bring into my life. If I want a friend, I must be a friend. If I want more love, I must give more love. In order to be a friend, or give more love, I must change.

I must learn to be a different and better person. I must learn to look for what is right in the world, in others, and in me. When I find it, I must nurture it and help it to grow.

If I do not have seeds, I cannot plant a garden. I must find things that I think are right and good. To do so I must search for them. If I do not look, I will not find. I must remember that what I look for, be it right or wrong, I will find—just like in the story of the two dogs to which I alluded earlier. Therefore, I must be diligent to keep my search positive and search for what is right and good.

Keeping my search on a positive note can do two important things for me.

First, it can help me identify things I consider good or right for me. It can help me focus on living in the solution, instead of in the problem.

Second, it can help me identify patterns of negativity in my life so that I can root them out and work to change them. This can be a long process of learning, but I can take it slow and work on the things I find directly in front of me. My challenge is to keep an open mind to what is without worrying about whether things will go my way or whether I will get what I need. And as I've proved to myself time after time, what I'm sure I need often turns out to be what I only think I need. In fact, I often discover that what I thought I needed is only what I wanted. Big difference.

When it looks like I am not making any progress, I must continue to participate and allow the process to continue. I sometimes feel that fear is really the absence of trust. As long as I do my part, while not insisting that I get my way, and as I gain more trust, I find that I feel less fear and gain more confidence.

## Pushing the Limits—Passing the Tests

I find my limits through adversity and fear. I must learn to push myself beyond where I think I can go. God will stop me before I reach beyond my limits if

I am paying attention. Then again, I might decide that I want to take a step back on my own. Sometimes growth seems too hard, my fears too great, or I just don't feel ready for a change. I have found it beneficial in these situations not to quit. I can scale things back a bit if I need to. I can slow down or work at an easier pace. I should never quit. I say this for one very important reason: because it relates back to making adjustments.

I have heard it said that God doesn't change people; God changes circumstances. I have used this as food for thought on many occasions when I wondered, "Why would God treat me this way?"

What I discovered when I began paying more attention was that I was receiving new opportunities to change and to meet life's needs. God was giving me a test. If I passed the test, I would not have to take it again. However, if I refused to take the test, if I tried to ignore it, or if I simply failed in my attempt, I would receive another, probably more difficult opportunity. This relates directly to when I reminisce about my past using days. I noticed that I received several opportunities to discover that I had a problem, yet I ignored them, refused them, or failed to attempt to change—to quit self-destructing. God changed my circumstances until I was finally able to see, beyond any doubt, that I needed to change.

I was one of the fortunate ones because I got sick of the consequences before using killed me. I finally became willing to do what was necessary to make a dramatic change in my life—to quit self-destructive behaviors. If I can do that, I can make other necessary changes as well. In addition, the best thing is that once I make the changes, I never have to go back to the old way of living again.

Once I pass a test, I am finished with that test. As long as I don't decide to go back to my old way of living, I should not have to take that test again. I have gone through the trials and tribulations of quitting my using, and now that I am in recovery, I don't ever have to use or act out again. Oh, I can go back to it, but that would be a choice at this point—a very bad choice, but a choice nonetheless. The same is true with other changes I make, other tests I pass, and other tasks I complete.

Take the example of testing my patience and tolerance that I discussed earlier. Those who arrive late to meetings I attend no longer annoy me. I rarely notice them except to see if they are someone I know, to give a wink and a nod, or to smile at them. I do these things to help relieve any anxiety that their tardiness may be causing, whether the anxiety rests in them, in me, or in someone else. After all, I have learned that there are much worse things than being late to a meeting. In fact, I have learned that we are only late to our first recovery meeting. I have learned that half a meeting is still a meeting and is better than no meeting at all.

Meetings are a lot like holes: half of a hole is still a hole. Meetings fill holes in my life. Before I started going to meetings or doing other recovery-related activities, I tried to fill the holes in my life with whatever substances or behaviors I could find. I lacked patience and used substances and behaviors to bring me what I thought I needed immediately. That stopped working, and so in early recovery I learned I needed many lessons in patience and tolerance. That first lesson in patience and tolerance—the woman who habitually arrived late to the meeting I attended—is still paying big dividends today. I received the dividends whether or not I was consciously aware of it. Of course, I am not immune to instances where life tries my patience. That is how life is, and I accept it. It would be foolish of me to think differently. There is always room to grow, and I will never be perfect concerning my patience. Improvement on my part is still a choice that I choose to make. I have made progress. Now I keep my eyes open for more opportunities to test my limits, to discover new tests to pass and new opportunities to improve.

Since I live with myself twenty-four hours a day, I figured it would be smart to get to know who I live with. I say this because when I first got into recovery, I had little idea who I was. Getting to know myself is something I will do for the rest of my life. However, now that I am paying attention, I am getting to know myself pretty well. In fact, I have learned something funny, yet interesting, about myself. Since I learned it by noticing it in others first, I now look for things in myself that I find in others. I recall an incident that was funny.

I was sitting in a meeting with my sponsor. He was old and had been in the fellowship for many years. I had asked him at one point how many people he sponsored, and he said, "Hundreds claim me."

I asked him what that meant, and he said that he heard some people say he was their sponsor in meetings, but that they never called him or used him as a sponsor. I decided they simply liked being associated with him because he had been around so long, and he let it go at that.

One day we were sitting in a meeting and a person said, "My sponsor, Chauncey, says . . ." and he went on to say something else. I don't remember what was actually said, but it sounded nothing like what I had ever heard Chauncey say. Confused, I leaned over and asked him if he sponsored the man. When he said that he didn't even know him, I asked if he had ever said what was attributed to him. Again, he said no; he didn't remember saying anything like it. I then asked if he planned to say anything about it to the person.

"No," he said. "It sounded pretty good to me. I'll take credit for it."

On the way home we got to talking about the incident, and he told me that many times people don't hear what you say. They hear what they need to hear. I thought about that and knew he was right. I remembered speaking in a meeting one time, and halfway around the table someone said something like "I like what Mark said," then he went on to say something I didn't say. However, others at the meeting liked what they heard. Who am I to argue with them? I had reacted to that situation just as my sponsor had reacted to what had happened this night.

Then there was the time when I went up to a guy after he had given an open talk to thank him for something he had said during the talk—something I found to be quite profound. When I mentioned it, he looked a little confused, then smiled, shook my hand, and said thank you. As this image floated up in my brain, I realized I had probably misheard him. I mentioned the incident to my sponsor and he said, "I often do not hear what is said, but if I listen closely, I will hear what I need to hear."

I am no longer afraid of misquoting what someone tells me in a meeting. It might not be what he or she said, but it is what I heard. What I heard is what is important. Nowadays I use what I heard to better myself and to help others. To me, it now makes perfect sense. I think this is how new understandings are forged. One person says something; another person hears what he or she needs to hear, even though it isn't what was said; and then apply it to his or her life and use it to help others see things in a different light.

I shouldn't complain about any of this, because it is hard enough to take advice—even if it is my own advice. Therefore, any time I can take some good advice, I should take it for a test drive and see what happens.

## Keeping It Simple

I remember a man I met in a meeting who shared almost the same thing every week. It didn't matter what the topic of the meeting was; he said the same thing, week in and week out. For a while I was somewhat perturbed by his repetition, even downright annoyed, but I soon realized he was doing what he knew. It was keeping him in recovery. How could I argue with what he was doing if it was helping him? I could not. I had to stop asking myself why he was the way he was and ask myself what I could do with what he offered. I parlayed that learning into something bigger for myself.

I should not ask, "Why am I the way I am?" but instead I should ask, "What can I do with what I have today?" The man who repeated himself each week at the meeting was staying in recovery. He kept coming back, and what he did was working for him. He was using what he had and doing what he needed to do. This was a simple lesson for others and yours truly. Sometimes I simply don't have the proper tools, but I need to get something done. I have used a screwdriver as a hammer before because I didn't have a hammer. Sure, it puts unnecessary wear and tear on the screwdriver, but it gets the job done. I think the same is true with my recovery. I can use the best tool I can find until I find a better tool. It just makes sense.

Even if I don't have the proper tool for a given situation, I can use what I have to stay on the road to recovery. If all I figure out today is don't use or act out in a negative way, I can use that. Even if what I am dealing with is resentment, until I learn how to deal with resentment I can just not act out. That simple understanding will keep me on the right path.

As I move forward, I will learn through trial and error that I need a new and better tool to deal with something new and challenging that has come up in my life. It is at times like these that I need to ask for help. I seem incapable of doing so, but I don't want to break my screwdriver by using it as a hammer, either. I know I need to get a hammer. I know I need to find someone who has a hammer and ask him where and how he got it. I usually know I need a new tool because what I am doing isn't working as well as it could or should. I may be chock full of fear or uncomfortable in some other way. When I recognize I am out of sorts, I need to ask for help. There is good reason for asking, too.

I have learned, through asking for new tools, that I may already have the necessary tools. I just don't know how to use them properly. I had to learn to use the screwdriver; I had to learn how to use the hammer. There are still tools I don't know how to use, but today I am willing to learn. I know that I am going to make some mistakes along the way. I have hit my thumb with a hammer more than once, but I still use a hammer. The same is true with the other tools of life.

I am still working on my intuition. Sometimes it is right on and sometimes it fails me. It usually causes me fear when it fails me or is wrong, so I am learning to heed that fear and learn from it. Fear can be my friend in times like these, because when I intuitively know how to do something, that's one matter; but when I think I know how to do something and I believe it is my intuition telling me, I usually feel hesitant, thanks to my fear. Intuition is a tricky tool, but one I need to practice using. It will help me to pay close attention to myself, to how I feel and what I am thinking and feeling in the moment. Living in the moment is always a good opportunity for me to learn. When I learn to pay close attention to myself, I can better deal with life in general because I learn whether I have the correct tools, need to learn to use new tools, or need help doing something I don't know how to do that I may never need to do again.

What is most important is that I need to keep things as simple as possible. The guy who said the same thing every week was using what he knew. For him, it works! While I haven't seen him in a few years, I hope he is doing well, and I hope he has picked up a few new tools in his travels through life and his recovery. Life seems more interesting when I have more tools to use in my tool bag.

The best tool I have is to recognize that every morning I wake up as a newcomer. As a newcomer, I must be ready and willing to learn. If I don't use or act out in some other way, and I learn something during the day, I go to bed a long-timer. I get to add just that one day to all the other days I have, and tomorrow I get to do it all over again. Staying in the solution and continuing to learn new things gives me that kind of experience. Then I can pass that experience on to others as others have passed it on to me. I get more experience by giving away my own. That is just the way it works, but it does work, as long as I do my part.

## 04 | Thinking It Through

**M**y brain is a tool. I need to learn how to use it. For far too long my brain told me what to do, how to act, whom to hang around with, and what kind of crazy things to do. My problem for the longest time was learning to use something I had never spent much time trying to use before. During my active addiction, I let alcohol and other drugs do my thinking for me. The rest of the time, I let my brain run free. Like a wild animal, it stalked its prey as it saw fit, sending me into some crazy, sometimes life-threatening situations. Like many people in recovery, I should have been dead a long time ago. I attribute this to the fact that I never used my brain properly. I still at times wonder why I am still here when my brain had it in for me for so long. Oh, I asked my brain for a favor on occasion. I would make a visit to my brain in order to remember something or to make a grocery list. There were many things I asked my brain to do for me, but mostly, I treated my brain like a king, while I was its loyal servant. Since I was afraid of my brain, it took advantage of my fear. Because of fear, my brain could run amok, like a child without discipline. In addition, it usually acted like a child without discipline, causing me to act the same way. I have worked to change that. I have learned to use my brain in a more positive way. Of course, I am still learning, but I have a much better grip on things nowadays.

I used to fear going into my head alone, because being alone in my head could be very dangerous. Today I don't go it alone. The difference between those fear-filled days of yesterday and my joyous today is that I have learned that my brain is a tool that I can and should know how to use to my advantage. Of course, just knowing this didn't alleviate the fear. I had to do a lot of work before the fear began to subside. By the time I decided to make strides into this area, I had already learned that fear is part of the process of growth and that I should work through the fear. I proceeded—cautiously at first—and finally figured out that I can put my brain to good use if I make it a habit and continue to work on it.

In my first book, *Becoming Normal: An Ever-Changing Perspective*, I focused on thinking. I spent nearly a quarter of the book telling others of tricks I have learned to use to get my brain to work for me instead of the other way around. A lot of trial and error went into those tricks, as well as a great deal of help from my sponsor and other trusted friends. However, the key point is that I did the work. I made it a daily practice to put my brain to use in ways I considered constructive. I did this because I figured that since my brain made so many decisions—decisions that brought actions and consequences—I should be involved in this decision-making process more than I had been.

Today, for the most part, I tell my brain what to think and how to spend its time. When it protests, and it still does on occasion, I remind it that I am the one running the show now and that I will tell it what is important to think about and what decisions need to be made.

At first, my brain was like one of my old friends—the ones who liked to party. I would tell it what I wanted it to do, and it would laugh at me and tell me things like "You can't do that. Let's go party." I wanted to listen to it, mostly because I had been listening to my brain for so long that it was what I knew how to do, even if it was not in my best interest.

Fortunately, I had good people to help me through those early days when my brain still rebelled at my telling it what to do. It was a bumpy ride, but I had good people who helped me over the rough spots. Unfortunately, my brain had some serious tricks up its sleeve. It raced around from thought to thought without spending enough time on any one thought for me to get a hold on anything solid or concrete. This kept me off balance for a while, but I figured out a way to beat it at its own game, and I slowed down the rapid-fire thinking.

Slowing the mind down and removing idle mind chatter allows me more serenity and creativity, so as my mind slowed down, I was able to get more time to use it for my own fiendish plan of a takeover. It was a slow process, and I still work at it today, but it has paid off in ways I could never have imagined. Slowing down my brain is a daily exercise. Today I have a brain that not only works, but also works on what I tell it to work on, without a major protest. That's not to say that my brain doesn't protest or think awful thoughts on occasion; it certainly does. It just doesn't do it as often. When it does throw a fit, I can tell it that I don't want to hear it and make it change what it is thinking. Life is so much simpler now that I can't imagine how I got by before I decided to learn how to use my brain instead of allowing it to use me.

I am going to give some examples of how I use my brain, but I didn't just wake up one day with the ability to do this. I learned how to do this over time, using tricks and exercises I describe in *Becoming Normal*.

When I come home from a party or other gathering where I meet with other people, and my brain wants to tell me that I acted like a fool, I tell it that I know better and will not listen to these accusations. I know my brain is programmed to put me down, and I must not allow it to do so. I disregard any negative feedback coming from my brain unless I decide it might do me good to analyze it more carefully. I do not let my brain tell me I made an idiot of myself. I tell it that I do not act like an idiot anymore—I haven't for some time now—and I won't allow my own brain to bad-mouth me.

As I see it, I have three options. The first two are that I can rehash the event, looking for anything I did that might have been embarrassing, or I can tell my brain to think about something else. Either way, the choice is mine. With practice and a little patience, I can choose whichever I want. When I decide to rehash the event to look for embarrassing antics, I can do so with objective detachment to feel good about my conclusion.

The third option—I usually pick this one no matter which of the other two I choose first—is to talk to others at the gathering about how much fun we had. If I am feeling particularly self-conscious about something I did or didn't do, I can ask one of my friends about it. I get good feedback these days, compared to what I used to get, when I ask my friends about my behavior at public gatherings. If I find out I did do something wrong, I know I can make amends and learn from my mistake.

Knowing I did well reinforces the fact that I can act normally.

Knowing I can make amends when I make a mistake gives me something to fall back on when my humanness causes me to act inappropriately. Both of these things are important when it comes to letting my brain know who is boss. The more my brain begins to believe that I am the boss, the less it tries to drive me crazy with its incessant chatter; the less it chatters, the more I can get it to do what I want.

I will admit this was a scary proposition when I first tried it, but fear is part of the process—especially any new process—and by working through the fear, I accomplished two things with these exercises. I gained more control of my brain and I became more able to work through my fears, including my fear of making decisions.

My fear of making decisions, I discovered, stems from the fact that I used to be able to blame my bad choices on my drinking. Right or wrong, for better or worse, my general comeback to doing something stupid was "Well, I was under the influence at the time." This excuse might not have appeased anyone else, but it usually made me feel better. I learned to lean on this excuse when I needed something to bail me out of a bad choice. Even if I only told myself I was loaded at the time—because I knew it wouldn't patch anything up with anyone else—I still did it to calm my nerves about making a bad decision.

When I was using, I could blame my mistakes on my using. Today I don't have that option. I must take responsibility for my actions. While this is good and right, it is also troublesome. Fear lives in my loss of excuses. Not having my excuse of being loaded at the time requires that I stand up and face the consequences of my actions. Because I cannot blame my mistakes on using, I have learned to be careful in my decision-making process.

Of course, I have made some mistakes in recovery where afterward I wished I could have said, "But I was loaded at the time," simply because they were horrible, miserable mistakes I wanted to, but could not, take back. I feared what people would think of me. My brain ran in circles, looking for ways to bash my self-esteem with sledgehammers of fear. What people would think of me seemed to be the major, number-one-with-a-bullet fear. But actually, there were many, many other fears on my brain's "hit" parade.

One time I made a mistake—a bad one—and I had to face the consequences without the help of a good excuse, or at least one I could live with. This is a very uncomfortable place to be. Even after facing the consequences, I still feel uncomfortable admitting my faults and mistakes without anything to say other than "I made a mistake."

Fear can be a useful tool, motivating me to change. I can use my fear of making a fool of myself to help me make better choices and decisions. Thanks to fear, I have learned to say no more often, or at least to ask for time to think about something before I plunge in headfirst without due consideration.

When someone asks me to help him or her, I take time to think about it. Before I dive in, I check the depth of the water to make sure it is sufficient for me to make a safe dive. Life may not be as spontaneous as before, but it is a lot safer—and a lot more comfortable. I have learned that my brain takes time to process things. Thinking is a process. Like a computer, my brain needs time to do its job properly. When the little box comes up on my computer that says, "One moment please," I let it work. Today I give my brain that same consideration and give it time to work.

If I have an important decision to make, I tell my brain to go think about it and report back. I have come to expect that it will get back with me. My general rule is, if someone asks me for something, my answer is no, until I can take some time to think about it. After I have given my brain the information it needs to make a decision and time to process it, my answer might change, but until I have taken what I consider an appropriate amount of time to ponder possible outcomes, I refuse to skip through the decision-making process.

My brain used to skip through the decision-making process like a child skips through a summer day. However, I am grown-up now and I need my brain to make grown-up decisions. When I was in active addiction I really could not make grown-up decisions, and instead allowed alcohol, drugs, and bad choices to make many of my decisions for me. Then I blamed the results on the alcohol, drugs, and bad choices. My fear of making bad choices has helped me to improve my decision-making process by slowing it down. My fear of not having a good reason for making bad choices has also helped me to make better decisions.

Since I know I can't make good, solid choices on my own all the time, I have learned to ask for guidance when I have to make tough decisions. If I don't know the answer, I ask my brain for a list of people who could help me make the necessary decision. When my brain reports to me with the list of people, I don't hesitate to ask one or more of the people listed. I would rather ask a friend for help and have him or her think I am silly for needing his or her guidance than make a bad choice and afterward look like a fool in front of the world.

## What We Think, We Become

The Buddha said, "What we think, we become." Today I believe that, so I am much more careful about what I allow my brain to think. When negative thoughts come into my head, I politely ask them to leave. If they are persistent, I order them out. If they ignore my order, I allow them to find an out-of-the-way corner of my mind to occupy where they can try to come up with a reason why I might want to give them an audience. Generally, though, a negative thought cannot come up with a good reason for me to dwell on it, so the thought will leave on its own.

Since my thoughts, words, and actions are the seeds that will bring forth the harvest of my future, I must begin today to fill my conscious mind with ideas of abundance and positive energy. Negativity has no place in my head unless it can provide me with constructive criticism that will help me to become a better person.

While I now see most fears as positive-negative thoughts, I still do not allow fear to run rampant in my head. I still check my fear to see if it might provide a constructive outcome before I let it live in my mind. While I have come to know that fear is a tool I can use to help me focus on my goals, to help me do a good job, or for many other good reasons, I still look for the harm it can cause me before I give it rent-free space in my head. After all, that rent-free space could cost me dearly if I don't do some checking first.

My general rule when dealing with my thoughts is, "When a thought arrives, acknowledge it, determine whether it is positive or negative, then treat it as such." In the process, I am making judgment calls on what I believe to be good or bad, which is something I don't like to do about things that happen in life, but when it comes to my thinking, I have found it to be an essential part of the process.

One reason I don't like to put good and bad labels on things is because I thought quitting drinking was the worst thing that could happen to me. Little did I know at the time that it would turn out to be the best thing I ever did.

While I do my best not to be too judgmental about things on the surface, I have discovered that I do know right from wrong, and I have come to trust my ability to make these determinations. Even in my using days, I knew right from wrong for the most part. I simply was unable to do right, or stop myself from doing wrong, based upon the fact that it was right or wrong. My addiction stood in the way. In fact, my using told me I should keep using, even though I knew the way I used was wrong.

Therefore, instead of focusing on what is good or bad or right or wrong, I now do my best to focus on what I want to become and who I want to be. If what I think about is what I will become, I focus my efforts on becoming who I want to be.

Of course, this leads me right back to my labels, because I want to be a good person who does the right things. However, I don't focus on the right or wrong or good or bad in me, but instead on who I am.

When I first got into recovery, I did not know who I was. I had acted so erratically for so much of my life that there was no way to know how I might act in any given situation, let alone know who I was deep down inside me. I felt I knew right from wrong, but was just as apt to do wrong as right. I felt I knew the good from the bad, but as it turned out, I was wrong enough times that I often was not sure.

I decided that I needed to get to know myself in order to determine what changes I needed to make so that I might become the person I always wanted to be. The most amazing thing that happened during the getting-to-know-myself process was that I changed. As I began to watch what I was thinking, throwing out what I didn't like and was taking up space in my head, I became a better person. As I became a better person, I found more things I didn't like roaming the halls of my head, reducing the efficiency of my mind, and I threw them out, too. It all started with throwing out what I considered, at the time, to be negative thoughts. Since what I think is what I will become, I decided to do away with negativity in my head in order to do away with it in other areas of my life. I decided fear was one of these negative thoughts, and began discarding it as fast as I could. This is when I discovered that fear is part of the process. It wouldn't leave; it seemed to linger. As I watched, I found fear might shrink somewhat, but it would never vanish completely. Fear would nag at me to do the right thing and to do my best. It would also nag at me, telling me that I would never be able to keep up the work I was doing to help me change my way of life.

I redoubled my efforts at living life one day at a time because my fear told me I could not keep it up forever. Sure, I made plans for the future, but I did my living, as often as I could, in the here and now. Fear has little presence in the here and now. I may fear an upcoming event, but the fear leaves me as soon as I participate in the event. I have given several speeches in recovery and I always get nervous or scared beforehand, depending on the speech and setting; however, any fear I may have floats out the window as soon as I begin the talk. I am convinced that this is because as I speak I am in the moment.

I cannot give a speech while thinking about something else. I must focus completely on what I am thinking and saying. I am so in the here and now that fear can't reach me.

I did the same thing with my life. I do my best to live in the now—to be so involved in what I am doing, as I am doing it, that when fear creeps in, I know it right away. Mindfulness is simple, but not easy. It takes practice. Even with practice, the future and the past like to barge in uninvited. Today I check them at the door to see what version they may be representing. If it is a version meant to cause me anguish or regret, I show them the door. In this moment, life is good. I need to live here and now.

Using my labels as a guide, I have done my best to stop focusing on what is wrong and focus on what is right with my life, on what is good about life and not what is bad. Focusing on what is wrong or bad robs me of a real quality of life I could be enjoying. Today I focus on what I can do, not on what I can't do.

I used to spend all my time dwelling on what I could not do, what life had robbed me of, what I had lost or given away, and I gave away a lot, so there was a lot to think about. I have discovered the truth behind the old cliché, "Every cloud has a silver lining." Every problem I have, or have had in my life, shows me and gives me an opportunity for growth—an opportunity to help someone else, an opportunity of some type. It is my job to find the hidden opportunity provided by what I used to think I lacked. The lack of things in my life used to rule me. Today I see a perceived lack of anything as a chance to grow. Fear cannot penetrate a positive attitude with much power or authority. A positive attitude does not make me invincible, but with it, I no longer do what I used to do or get what I used to get.

## Every Thought Is a Prayer

I heard in a meeting, "Every thought is a prayer," and it scared me. When I looked at the thoughts running through my head, it scared me a lot. I decided I was praying a lot of negativity and that I needed to change. I decided to pay attention to what I was thinking and not allow my fear and self-criticism to dominate my thoughts. It was a lot of work, all of it mental, but it has paid huge dividends. Now my thoughts are more positive, more productive.

For me to think "right thoughts" takes a lot of thinking. I have actually started a practice I call "meditate on every moment." It is another one of those "easier said than done" opportunities. While it is likely impossible to meditate on every moment, I call it that because it reminds me to take my time with my thinking. It helps me remember not to smash the monitor in my head when it says, "One moment please," because my brain needs time to work. Instead, I take that moment to take a breath, relax, and give myself a mental break.

Since my brain is capable of so much, while I am taking this little mental break I can check to see how the rest of me is doing. What am I feeling? What else am I thinking of? Am I on schedule for the day? As these productive thoughts are taking place, I am giving my brain some peace (if only for a second) to work on the main problem, so it can think it through and give me options.

I have found it best to give my brain as much time as possible to do what it needs to do, disturbing it only if I have to, while it is working on that most important thought. That is not to say that I stop thinking, or that I even try to. What I do is try to stop thinking about the particular thing that I am having difficulty dealing with.

I always try to do this with big decisions, and I do it with my writing. When I find myself on the verge of an impulse buy, or when there is a large sum of money involved, I do my best to delay any decisions that concern spending the money for a minimum of three days. This gives me time to consider whether I actually need to make the purchase or not. As for my writing, I prepare my brain for tomorrow's writing as soon as I finish my writing today. Then I let it think about tomorrow's topic for the rest of the day, and possibly as I sleep. This works well for me, since I do my writing in the morning and I usually find that when I wake up, the topic or idea that I wanted my brain to think about has cleared and coalesced into a coherent and easily understood course of action.

While these are examples of things I am allowed the luxury of spending my time thinking about, often—at least it seems so to me—my mind wants to press me into a quick decision. I have found that, even during these times, I am better off giving myself a short break to think. When I can't find my car keys, if I take a moment to stop and think rather than run around looking in the next place I happen to think of, I can often find them much more quickly. Simply taking a seat and doing some deep-breathing exercises can help me calm my mind enough to remember where I left them.

When it comes to people trying to pressure me into doing something I may or may not want to do, I have discovered that if I simply make my first answer a "no"—if only in a faint voice in my head and not aloud—it allows me time to think before I give my final answer. Saying no to myself creates a brief internal debate on the request: "Should I or shouldn't I?" With an immediate, although internal, no, negative, etc., my brain is able to look at the request and come up with reasons why I should or shouldn't go and do whatever is being asked of me. If I simply answer yes, I do none of this internal debate; I give my answer, and off we go. These automatic reactions are what used to get me into all kinds of trouble.

This was especially true during my many years in active addiction. Even in early recovery, I used to say yes all too often to things that sounded like a good idea at the time. Without any consideration as to possible consequences, I would jump at nearly any offer made, regardless of who made the offer or how crazy it may have sounded. I include myself as one of the architects of some of these wild and crazy schemes, because I had some of the worst ideas and simply acted on them without thinking. This is, I believe, where "I wasn't thinking" came from. "I wasn't thinking" isn't much of an excuse. Today I believe it ranks right up there with "But I was loaded at the time."

Training myself to give my brain the time needed to do its job was a process in and of itself. In the beginning, I didn't even trust myself to do that right. After all, I can't fix a broken thinker with a broken thinker. A computer with faulty programming cannot run a diagnostic and correct its own programming. It needs outside help. Like the computer, I cannot fix my thinking all by myself. If I could, I would. Life just does not seem to work that way. If it did, I would not have had so many problems in my life, including my addiction.

In early recovery, rather than simply allowing myself time to think, I would call my sponsor or another trusted friend and talk to them about whatever was troubling me. Doing so automatically stopped me from making snap decisions.

I knew I was making progress in this area when someone offered me the job of revamping the helpline. As soon as someone made the offer to me, I knew I would take the job, but my immediate answer was "I'll have to talk to my sponsor. I'll let you know tomorrow." That night, when I called my sponsor, I told him about the opportunity and that I had told the person that I would talk it over with my sponsor.

My sponsor said, "You'll probably fall on your butt and make a fool of yourself."

"Well," I stammered, "You have taught me that when that happens, I should just get up and dust myself off and move on."

"Take the job," he said. "You'll do fine."

Then I slept on it anyway. Before I went to sleep, I told my mind to come up with ways to get the job done. In the morning, I had an idea. It wasn't much, but it was a start. As time went on I kept that thought in the back of my mind, working all the time with orders to report any new progress. The ideas kept coming. As I talked to my sponsor (who had experience in this area) and with other people who had been working the helpline, things started taking shape.

Another positive result that comes from taking my time with my thinking is that I allow contact with God on the matter. I am getting better at praying about things *before* I do them. I used to use prayer as a last resort. Today I do my best to pray first. I have come to believe that by saying even a quick prayer, like "God help me," I end up making better choices. My thinking is much clearer on the matter because I not only give my brain time to do its job, but I reach out for help from the ultimate power in my life. There has been another unexpected bonus to this practice: I have rediscovered my intuition.

When I was using, I thought intuition was the first thing that popped into my head. Today I see intuition as the ability to tune into my innate wisdom, to that part of me connected to God. I see my ability to tune into this wisdom as a direct result of asking for the help of my Higher Power . . . the ultimate power of the universe.

One of the promises laid out in recovery program literature is "We will intuitively know how to handle situations which used to baffle us." However, it doesn't say it will just happen automatically. It says we will have to work for it. While I see my intuition today as something that comes from God, I also see it coming from my life experience. Just as a cake needs several key ingredients, so does my intuition require more than one ingredient to give the right answer. Like baking a cake, it takes practice to do it right consistently. As I practice using my newly found intuition, I make mistakes, and that is okay by me. When I fall on my butt, I get up and dust myself off, I make my amends, and I move on.

This was very scary stuff when I first began to work with my intuition and my thoughts. It can be scary today even with some experience. I can't hide from my thinking, so I need to stand up to it—even though it may scare me. In the process, I get more than I bargained for. I learn to think better, and in the process I overcome some of my fears. Learning to use my brain has been, and continues to be, a process that at times fills me with fear, yet one that is also full of promise and rewards.

One of the reasons learning to use my brain can fill me with anxiety is that I know all my secrets—they like to roam the halls in my head like bullies and ghosts. I know all the bad things I have done, all the times I have acted on thoughts, causing problems either for myself or for others. However, knowing all of my secrets can be a good thing too, because I know my secret strengths. The key to overcoming the fears I have about learning to use my brain is to focus on these strengths and use them to surmount the old bad habits. I do this by changing the way I live my life, I do this by changing the way I act, and I do this by changing how and what I choose to think.

As I begin to think properly, and do it more and more consistently, I make fewer bad choices. As I make fewer bad choices, I begin to live a more positive, life-enhancing existence. I become a productive member of society rather than being the drain I used to be on the lives of those around me. Eventually, my good deeds and positive thoughts outweigh my bad secrets. Like any process, this change takes time. It may take years, but the rewards will come. Unless I die today, I have the time for this change. I must simply begin to put my time to good use, and the best use of my time that I can think of is to begin to do what is necessary to build a strong, positive thinking habit, and then add to it every day.

When I was using, my thinking was a big part of my problems. Today it is the source of my solutions. I need to treat it properly. I need to do whatever is necessary to change the way I think, the things I think about, and the actions brought about by my thinking, from the negative, fear-based way I used to live into a strong, positive, new way of thinking and living. In order to do this I must move through my fear of change, which tells me that I can't do it or that it will not work, and I must practice making my brain do work for me.

## 05 | Getting Honest

Honesty is part of the foundation of my recovery program. It is but one cornerstone, and, joined by open-mindedness and willingness, it provides me a solid foundation without which I risk returning to some of my old destructive ways, which led me down the path of addiction. Of the three cornerstones, I consider honesty to be the most important. Without honesty, I have little chance at staying open-minded and willing. Without honesty, I may tell myself that I am open-minded and willing when, in actuality, I am not. Honesty causes me the most fear, or so it seems.

The reason honesty used to cause me so much fear is that I thought being honest meant that I had to tell the truth, the whole truth, and nothing but the truth, all the time. I felt I had to be completely honest even if it meant I might hurt myself or hurt others. I have found this to be an erroneous conclusion, concocted by fear, to keep me dishonest or to keep me from approaching the kind of honesty I needed to build a life based upon honesty that would be the key not only to recovery, but also to the good, solid life I could enjoy.

Today I know more about honesty. I know there is a middle-of-the-road approach I can adopt. This approach can keep me in recovery, sane, and happy. The middle-of-the-road approach that I am talking about consists of me being brutally honest with myself. I need to build a thick enough skin to be able to face the world, and I need to know when I am trying to lie to myself, while being gentle with others.

Being brutally honest with myself means that I have to catch my disease when it tries to tell me lies—lies like "I can have just one," or "I am too different from others for any program to work for me." After a rather short time in my recovery program, I could easily identify these kinds of lies running around in my head before they could do their damage. The sneakiest lie was "It is okay to tell a lie." This one caused me the most trouble and was the hardest to identify. You see, this is the first lie I must tell myself, under any circumstances, in order to tell a lie. I must convince myself it is okay to lie in order to not only lie to others, but to tell myself a lie. Once I step onto this slippery slope, I can easily find myself telling, and listening to, the lie that says, "I can have just one"—of anything I know is bad for me. Once I figured this out, I decided I needed to know when my disease was trying to convince me to venture down the path of dishonesty. When my disease tells me it is okay to lie to you or to anybody else, it is simply trying to get me to take a step back into active addiction. This reason alone is good enough for me to want to overcome lying with honesty—brutal, unrelenting honesty—at least in my own heart and head. I have to know when I am trying to lie to myself. Once I know the truth about my tendency to lie, I can easily gauge when I am trying to tell a lie, or the truth, to someone else.

In *Becoming Normal: An Ever-Changing Perspective*, I talked about the difference between excuses and reasons. Here I want to talk about the similarities they share. The one huge similarity they have in common is that they can cause me problems with honesty. Regardless of whether I am giving an excuse or a reason for the lie, it may not be acceptable to the person I am giving it to.

I may have the best reason in the world for not wanting to attend some party or gathering that my friends want me to go to—my mother may be in the hospital and I plan to go see her instead. If my friends want me to join them, they might still try to talk me into going with them. To me it is a reason for not going, and to them my reason is an excuse. I know this today, and because of this I have learned that giving my reasons for not wanting to go somewhere or do something is unnecessary. Understanding that I do not owe anyone an explanation for my decision allows me to short-circuit the fear that surrounds the process of saying no—especially when saying no to my friends. Today, I do not offer excuses or reasons for not doing things or for saying no. Today I simply say no and stick by my decision. This was a difficult task when I first started doing it because I was conditioned to provide my reason or excuse for not wanting to do something. I used to feel as though I owed others the reason why I did or did not want to do something. Today I understand that I have freedom of choice and that I do not necessarily need to explain to anyone my reasons for making a decision.

For instance, if I was offered an opportunity to do something, whether it was going to a party or helping a friend build a deck on his house, I thought I had to have a good enough reason in order to decline. I thought I had to convince others that my reason was a good one. I don't anymore. Today I can say, "No, thank you," or "I'd rather not," and be done with it.

Sometimes people pry, and here is where my fear begins. My closest friends know better these days than to pry too deeply. They have learned over time, if they didn't already know, that I will only give my reasons—my real, full reasons—for not participating in some activity if I feel comfortable giving them. In addition, I only feel comfortable giving them if I am close enough to the person to know he or she will not badger me about the legitimacy of my reason. I usually tell the whole story to my closest friends. I do not fear them questioning my wants, needs, and desires, and ultimately my reasons.

There are people, though, to whom I will not give a reason. I do so to keep fear in its place, and its place is to serve as a tool. What an epiphany this was for me, using fear to help me relieve fear. I have devised a preprogrammed, canned response that I can give in any situation where I want to say no while keeping my reasons for doing so to myself. I keep this response handy, in my hip pocket, if you will, for those occasions where I want (or need) to say no and be done with it. My response is "I have other plans," or "I have another commitment." Although such responses may appear to be less than completely honest, I choose to use them instead of saying no because by doing so I do not have to explain why I am saying no. Some people can't take no for an answer and may want to know what my "other plans" are. And when I think about it I realize that I may actually have other plans; I just don't know what they are at the moment.

Fear is the tool I use to let me know when these responses might be necessary. When someone offers me an opportunity to do something, to provide a service, to make a commitment I may not be interested in, fear rises up in me. It does so because I am afraid he or she may reject my reason for not wanting to participate. It is a fear of rejection, a fear of what others might think, or a fear of losing my standing with this person (or these people) that motivates me to keep my canned response at the ready. What the fear *is* really doesn't matter; I point it out simply to show how it boils down for me. What matters is that fear rears its ugly head, and I usually think it is the fear of saying no that is the problem, when it is not.

When fear shows itself in this way, I need to use it to remind myself that I need not give my reasons (or even my excuses) in order to just say no. That is how I can use fear as a tool in situations like this. Fear can become an ally when I previously thought it was my enemy. When I use it properly, as I do now, fear can become my friend, one that kindly warns me to check myself before I speak. It can help me not put my foot in my mouth.

Sometimes people like to try to trick me into making a commitment before I even have a chance to say no or think about it. I am still learning to recognize this tactic as it is happening, but when I do, I have a way to deal with it as well. Here is an example:

Someone will ask, "What are you doing Friday?"

When I am on my toes, I recognize it for what it is, an attempt to discover my reasons and excuses before asking me to commit. If I say I don't have anything going on Friday, he or she has a clear shot at getting me to go along with whatever he or she wants me to do. There are two cures for this kind of "asking" that I have come across. One cure is to recognize it immediately for what it is; the other cure I save just in case I miss what is happening the first time around and have to cover myself.

If someone asks me what I am doing on Friday (or anytime in the future) I can simply say, "I don't know. Why?" Answering his or her question with a question allows me to take back the control I deserve to have over my schedule and my fear.

If I miss the opportunity on the front end and tell them I have nothing going on Friday, then find myself feeling trapped into doing something I would rather not commit to, I can still get out of it. This is more difficult to do. Fear can rise much higher, much faster, and tell me that I have no way out, that I must go along. The truth, however—and I know this is the truth if I am honest with myself—is that I can simply say no. I can do so in a way that allows everyone to save face and avoid feeling foolish, but I need more prepared responses in order to do so without hesitating, stumbling over my words, or blabbering on about my reasons.

My canned response is "I don't think I want to commit to that just yet. Let me think about it. I'll get back to you." If I add that last part, I need to remember to get back with that person, so sometimes I leave it off, depending on the person, as well as whether I think I may actually want to participate in the activity. Still, I have a response ready for just such an occasion. I have it as a defense against fear and as a useful tool to ward off those who try to "steal" my schedule. I use fear to let me know when it is time to use it.

Of course, not telling the whole truth is known as a lie of omission; I will not argue that point here. But I will make a case for restricting the amount of information I choose to share with others as a way of setting boundaries, or limits.

After all, my time on this planet is limited and valuable. I used up a lot of my time in unproductive ways during my active addiction. I must make up for lost time. Besides, my friends do not have to know everything about my life. My life is not an open book. I value the fact that they think so highly of me as to include me in their lives, but limits or boundaries are a necessary part of everyone's life. My friends understand, but that does not mean they will not test my boundaries.

The responses I have learned to use are honest; they are just not too honest. My goal is simply to balance my honesty—the honesty I have within myself—so it is important that I am okay with the whole process. If I think that telling other people only as much as I think they need to know about my reasons or excuses is not being honest, then I may well have a problem with my honesty. For now, though, telling others only so much works for me. Honesty is, after all, a two-way street, and it comes in increments. I would not tell a complete stranger my life's story, and I don't believe a stranger would or should tell me his or hers. As I get to know someone, gain more comfort and more trust, I may open up more. The point is that not opening up too quickly or not sharing too much information is not lying, even though some people may think it is. Then, if they keep digging too deep, I have to ask myself, "What are their true motives?" I will discuss honesty later.

For now, I say I do not want to go down that road because I have enough things on my mind to think about. I like to keep it simple. If a friend is a true friend, he or she should be able to gauge or learn to gauge when it is time to stop digging and just accept my answer. After all, if I believe it is okay to keep my reasons to myself, yet I still think keeping my reasons to myself is lying, then I have a bigger problem. This can cause fear to grow, since I cannot keep my reasons to myself without feeling as though I am being dishonest; yet if I tell my reasons to others, I may be rejected. When this happens, I feel caught in a difficult situation. This is not where I want to be, because it feeds my fear. The bigger my fear is, the greater the chance is that I will not discover the appropriate level of honesty or that I may, in some way, compromise my privacy. I deserve my privacy. I keep my reasons to myself to maintain my privacy. Sharing too much information about the "why" or "why not" wastes valuable time and energy, and since my reasons will never please someone who really wants me to do what he or she asks me to do anyway, I might as well keep them to myself.

## The Truth Might Change, but Honesty Is a Constant

The truth can vary at times. While there are many truths that may never change—the sun always rises in the east, for example—some truths change occasionally. For instance, the best football team is decided each year because there is a new season and a new opportunity to discover which team is the best. Some truths are debatable (who is the best actor or actress?), while others depend on who witnessed the event and are based on their perception of what happened.

If four people stand on a street corner and watch as an accident occurs, you will end up with four different versions of the truth. Each person will see the accident from his or her perspective and tell a truth based on that perspective. While there is only one truth about what happened, all four people saw something different, and perceived a different truth. The drivers of the cars will also have differing truths about what happened based upon their own beliefs about what good drivers they are, bashing their own egos by admitting fault, or any number of intangibles. Still, there is only one set of circumstances that led to the collision. There is only one truth, but that truth is interpreted differently by those involved and those who witnessed it.

Does that mean the four witnesses are lying? I don't think so. I think they are telling what they believe to be true—if they are all being honest, and I am making that assumption here—even if all four people give accounts of the accident that clash as badly as the two cars did.

Because of this, I tend to believe that the truth can change from person to person and time to time. I used to think that when two people disagreed, one person had to be right and the other person had to be wrong. I now understand that two people can agree to disagree, and in that situation both parties are right. They are not bad people; they believe what is the truth for them. They just perceive things a little differently. That is okay. If everybody saw the world the same way, it would be a very boring world.

Another example of changing truth is how scientists show us how something is good for us one year, then change their mind the next year based on new evidence. An example of this is the almighty egg. At one point in time, the egg was not good for you. It was a source of cholesterol, which we needed to avoid. Now we see the egg as a good source of protein. Did the cholesterol leave? Did the egg somehow change its chemical makeup? No, but the benefits of the protein seem to outweigh the cholesterol, at least for those who do not have high cholesterol. The point is not whether eggs are good or bad for me; the point is that the truth can change over time as new evidence is discovered. The truth I choose to believe can change over time as well. After all, I did not analyze an egg in a laboratory; someone else did, and I base my truth on the facts or truth that I choose to believe, based on what others present to me. I need to be aware that the truth can change—even in my own life. My truths change based upon my beliefs. After all, if I believe something is right or true, that makes it right or true for me. I believe in God. I used to have my doubts (I still do occasionally). However, today I see how God works in my life and I use this evidence as proof that there is a God. My beliefs changed, and so did the truth—at least for me. Some people do not believe in God, and no one can change their mind about that. They may change on their own someday, but that is up to them. I cannot change it for them, nor will I try. What I have found to be most important here is that the truth can change. It can change for me even if it doesn't change for those around me.

Honesty, on the other hand, does not change. Honesty remains constant. Either I use it or I don't. I am either honest or I am not. Honesty is one place in my life where I have found that I can be all or nothing and it is a good thing, at least when dealing with my internal honesty. I am referring to my internal honesty only at this point. Honesty with others I have already discussed, but now I am getting down to the nitty-gritty of honesty. To be honest with myself is my first concern. If I cannot be honest with myself, then I cannot begin to be honest with others. Either I am being brutally honest with myself or I am not. There is no middle of the road when it comes to being honest with me. I cannot tell myself "little white lies" and think I am completely honest with myself. It no longer works for me. The reason it does not work is that the little white lies I tell myself put me on that slippery slope toward telling myself that "I can have just one" without causing myself any problems. The truth about this is that I have proven to myself that I can never "have just one" without causing problems. This is an unchanging truth, ranking right up there with the sun rising in the east, one truth I should not try to defy. I tried long enough and hard enough to "have just one" (or three or six) to know that I can't do that any more than I can stop the sun from rising in the east. Today I am honest enough with myself to know this truth, and I catch this lie quite easily when it tries to creep into my head.

When I pay attention to what I am thinking, I can catch every lie that tries to worm its way into my head. I can even catch the lie that tells me it is okay to lie to other people. I can stop myself from lying to other people while maintaining my own privacy and keeping my fear from making me crazy.

Therefore, while the truth may change, if I use honesty as completely as I possibly can, I can know when my truths change, when my beliefs change, and I can be honest about the fact that I am changing as a person. Through this honesty, I can allow myself to change and be true to my own personal growth.

Being honest can be hard for many reasons. One reason is that I must think. I must analyze what happens and report (to myself, at least) as accurate an assessment as I possibly can. This was especially hard when I first got into recovery, thanks to my years of practiced lying, deceiving, and manipulating. Practice anything—using, lying, *anything*—and you get good at it. It becomes second nature. Lying, deceiving, and manipulating were second nature to me until I changed my perception of what is normal and what I wanted my true nature to be. I had to relearn how to exist, begin to live, and continue to grow.

As I said, for a long time I didn't know how to be honest. It was something I had to learn, and learning something new can be difficult. However, with practice, I gained the ability to be honest, and once I did I discovered that it is much easier to be honest than it is to be dishonest. It is certainly safer for me to be honest, especially with myself, since being honest helps me stay in recovery. This reason alone led me to the willingness I needed to practice honesty until I had a good grip on how to do it. Since I have learned how to be honest, I have discovered that being honest is actually easier than lying. I can no longer place blame on my addiction. The main reason telling the truth is easier than lying is that even though to lie I can just make things up, I must then remember what I made up and who I told it to, as well as what really happened. It is difficult to remember old lies and prop them up with new ones. I cannot remember all those lies. When I tell the truth, at least as I see it, I only have to remember one version. If my truth ever changes due to my personal growth or the introduction of new evidence or for any other reason, I can laugh at myself for believing something that wasn't true. I tend to laugh at myself in these cases because it dilutes the fear that comes along with admitting the new truth, the fear that tells me I must always be right. The real, unchanging truth is that I can't always be right, because I'm human. Lying used to raise my level of fear exponentially. I was always afraid of being discovered for who I was. That was a terrible way to live, but at the time I could not figure out how to change it. Entering recovery was the first step toward change. I remember telling my mom, after being in recovery for some time and learning to be honest, that telling the truth was much easier than lying and easier than I ever dreamed of. I said something to the effect of "I can't imagine lying anymore; I have a hard enough time remembering the truth." As these words spilled from my mouth, I discovered how much simpler my life had become thanks to my newly discovered honesty. I didn't have to remember the truth, the lie, and whom I had told what—let alone remember whom I had told what when I told more than one lie about something. Now I simply had to remember what I believed the truth was and readily admit it when I thought I was mistaken about the truth. I could simply follow my convictions until I outgrew them; then I could adopt the new truth without too much fear about what others might think of me for changing my mind. I am growing and changing, after all, so why should I fear changing my beliefs or my truths?

When I decided to get honest, one of the hardest things I had to do was to figure out what lies I actually believed, or at least had believed, in order to begin to change how I thought about things. Some of them I knew. The lie about "having just one" was a glaring example of believing a lie. There were many others. I am sure you can come up with your own list of lies you believe. It probably won't be too different from mine. I had to search for the lies I believed. This was yet another reason why making the shift from lying to honesty was a tough sell to my tortured brain during early recovery.

One huge lie I believed was that I could never overcome fear. This lie was rooted in the fact that I believed courage meant the absence of fear. My truth, lie, or misguided thinking told me that courageous people didn't know fear. Fear never touched those who did courageous acts. My new truth surrounding fear is that courageous people do experience fear. They simply move through it, or deal with it, in a positive manner. Because of this, I have changed the way I think about fear, as well as the way I deal with it.

I now see fear as a tool to help me undergo the process of life. Fear crops up in so many ways that I doubt I could count them, yet I can learn to use that fear as a tool today. Sure, there are still times when I am scared out of my mind about doing something I know I must do. I doubt that will ever go away. It may be one of those unchanging truths. However, a new truth I have discovered is that these cases have been few and far between since I began facing fear head-on and moving through it.

Being honest has also helped me to move through fear. Being honest has reduced my level of fear. I have always been afraid of someone labeling me as a fraud. Since I no longer live a life of lying, cheating, and manipulating to get my way, I no longer fear being found out for these things. Oh sure, the fear crops up from time to time, but I know the truth about me now, and the truth is that I am a different person today. I know that the truth is just this: I used to be a bad person. I am a good person today, and the way I live my life today helps me deal with my past.

My biggest fear used to be that people would discover my sordid past and that I would never be good enough. These are quite simply a fear of the past and a fear of the future. The truth is that I have no control over either. The past is gone, and the future isn't here yet. I can do nothing for either of them except be the best I can right now.

Sure, someone can find out about my past, but at least he or she will discover the truth and that I am not lying now, today, in the present moment. I have many friends now who never knew me when I was active in my addiction and I was lying, cheating, and manipulating my way through life. For the most part, they could not care less about my past. In fact, occasionally, because they know about my past, they ask me to help their friends who have similar issues. What a wonderful blessing, getting to use my past to help someone else.

As for my future and my fear that I will never be good enough, the truth I have discovered is that I am already good enough. That, in and of itself, is scary, but I have found it to be true. I still doubt it sometimes, and I still try to improve a little each day. However, I have evidence to prove the point that I am good enough today, just for today. People ask me to help them; people ask me to help their friends. They must think I am good enough at least for that. I can help them thanks to my past. For me, today, that is good enough. As for whether I will be good enough in the future, there is only one sure way to ensure that I am. If I keep doing what I am doing to the best of my ability, and do what I can to become even better each day, I will keep getting what I am getting. The difference between now and when I was using is that I am moving in a positive direction. I continue to make improvements in my life. To continue to do the things I have done to get where I am and to continue to improve, being honest must play a big part in that process.

While dishonesty is wrong on so many levels, probably the biggest, most wrong thing—the thing that contributes to or strengthens my disease—is that dishonesty is selfish. Selfishness has caused so many heartaches in my life, and while not all of my selfishness stems from dishonesty, the part that does can cause me a lot of pain. Selfishness keeps me from doing things that are good for me (and those I care about) because I cannot see what I might get out of the act of giving. It makes me think too much of myself while I ignore others—or, worse yet, try to figure out ways to manipulate them into being or doing what I want them to be or do. To do this, I find myself tempted to do dishonest things. Fortunately, today, when I try to do something dishonest, fear will raise its ugly head. If I am paying attention, I can use this fear (usually fear of being found out, fear of what others will think of me, and fear of losing my good standing) to correct my behavior before I do something dishonest— before I lie, cheat, or try to manipulate others.

These days, I do my best to catch myself before I act dishonestly, because I have discovered that while the truth may hurt for a little while, a lie can hurt forever. The lie may not hurt right away. It may make things easier for the time being, until the truth comes out. However, when the truth does come out (as it nearly always does), the lie can ruin a relationship beyond repair. Since I base nearly all relationships on trust, when I lie and someone discovers me, I violate that trust. Sometimes the other person or people are willing to forgive me. Other times they are not and decide to leave the relationship, and, as I have discovered, this is not such a bad idea. In either case, trust is lost and the relationship damaged. Trust is not something I am willing to give up so easily anymore. It is too hard to build in the first place; it is even harder to rebuild. It is so much easier to be honest from the get-go.

A final thought about honesty brings me to the fact that when I lied (and I did a lot of it in my active addiction), I expected other people to lie as well. I have discovered that I usually expect other people to act the same way I do. When I was using, I thought everyone used. Now that I am in recovery, I seem to meet many other people in recovery. Even though I know there are many people who are not recovering from some form of addiction, it seems I find them everywhere. I have also found many people who choose not to use, and I have discovered that there really are people who use socially—whatever the substance is that they choose—and this revelation was a real shocker! As I have come to see that other people don't all act the way I do, I have also found that I still like to think they do, at least sometimes. Since I still do this, I prefer to think people are mostly honest. My mom has told me that I am a little too naive sometimes, that I trust people too much. However, I have decided that I would much rather get burned occasionally by those who are dishonest, because that means that I am being honest. If I were being dishonest, I would expect those around me to be dishonest as well, which would likely prevent me from being duped by their dishonesty, but at the price of my living a serene, relaxed life.

I don't go around believing everything people tell me. I have adopted the "trust but verify" mindset. If something sounds too good to be true, I check it out—and usually find it *is* too good to be true. However, I lean toward trusting people before they have earned it, then allowing them to live up to the trust I have given them. After all, there is only one other thing they can do, and that is to throw my trust away. I have learned to forgive more easily, so when they do decide to deceive me, I have a way to correct that as well. I can forgive them and move on with or without them in my life.

In the meantime, I am being honest to the best of my ability. In the process, I am living a life where fear has no real home.

I do not fear my past, because those who know me already know my past, and those who find out about it after meeting me can make up their own mind about whether or not they want to continue the relationship. When I meet other people, they usually find out rather quickly about my past and that I am in recovery. The amazing thing I have found is that most people think it is great that I am in recovery, especially those who knew me in my active addiction. I guess they make a quick comparison from what they know about addiction and conclude I am better off in recovery.

I need not fear my future, although I sometimes still fear what is to come, if I am being honest today. I can simply remind myself that as long as I am telling the truth now—as I believe the truth to be—then even if I change what I believe, all I have to do is admit that I believed something that turned out to be false. That is a whole lot easier than trying to cover my tracks as I used to do after telling a bunch of lies.

My honesty, while keeping my fear of the past and the future at bay, helps me live in the day and in the moment. I have found that living in the moment is the most comfortable thing I can do. After all, right this minute everything is fine. Most of the time things are fine.

Being as honest as I can, and being brutally honest with myself while being gentle with others, has given me a real sense of freedom from fear. It has also given me the opportunity to use fear as a tool—one I can even use to fend off fear itself. No wonder I consider honesty to be the most important of the three cornerstones of my recovery. With the right balance, honesty can give me the freedom I have been seeking my entire life.

# 06 | Expectations, Emotions, Experience, and Ego

I touched on this topic in my first book, but I believe it bears repeating with an emphasis on fear. After all, my expectations can cause fear to take hold of my life. If I have high expectations, my fear is that I will never achieve them. If I do my best to live without expectations (or have low expectations), I fear I may be missing out on something I want or need in this life; I might be letting myself and others down by not living up to my potential. Again, I can look to fear as a friend in this instance once I see the arrangement for what it is: an opportunity for growth.

In *Becoming Normal*, I said that I could have all the expectations I wanted as long as I have acceptance enough to meet the results. I stand by this statement, since my expectations push me to do my best while the acceptance tempers my ability to deal with the outcome. My job, after all, is to do my best at performing the task at hand. I may work toward a goal, but the results may differ wildly from what I expected to happen. Because the results may vary so dramatically, I have found that acceptance is a crucial ingredient in my everyday life. Consciously applying acceptance to my expectations only makes sense to me. In addition, the conscious application of acceptance to whatever happens when setting my expectations helps me to alleviate my fears around having my expectations set too high or too low.

Therefore, properly dealing with the fear that seeps into my life when I am setting my expectations is important, because it helps keep me grounded in reality while reaching beyond my limits. I have learned that I can use fear as a tool in determining when I am setting my expectations too high or too low. I can also use it to decide if I need to adjust my expectations, if I need to raise my level of acceptance, or if I need to do both. When fear rises inside me while I am trying to determine what my expectations should be or what I would like them to be concerning a particular goal, I can use that fear to help me find a reasonable level of expectation as well as the necessary level of acceptance to go along with it.

Writing is a tough business, but I love to write, so I must deal with my expectations and my level of acceptance on a conscious level. When I was writing my first book, I had the idea for this book. Fear made its familiar presence known. I hadn't even finished the first book, let alone found someone to publish it, and I was already thinking about this one.

How could I be thinking about the next book? Was I crazy? Fear told me that I was. Maybe it was right, at least to some extent. It can seem like asking for a miracle while trying to get a book published, especially when you haven't been published before.

I decided that I would deal with the fear by simply doing what I could do. Then I had to determine what it was, exactly, that I could do. At the time, I found the answer was so simple: I could continue to write the first book. I could expect that I would find a publisher and that the publisher would find it worthy of expending their resources and putting their name on it.

The amazing thing about this process is that I decided I would not work on accepting that the book wouldn't be published. I made a very conscious decision not to accept defeat, at least not until I thought I might have to. I found that I could have the willingness to find acceptance if I needed it, but that I certainly wouldn't accept defeat easily. I had high expectations, lofty goals, and a lesser willingness to accept defeat. Fear raised its head and told me again that I was crazy. Fear told me, "People get turned down all the time"; people told me the same thing. However, I spoke back: "People get published all the time too." I had to continue doing what I thought was right and wait to see what happened.

Still, the fear of writing a second book struggled to the surface. My answer to that fear was that I would deal with that when I got to it. After all, how can I write a second book if there is no first book? This logic applies to any situation, be it first book or first use of an addictive substance. I can't use the second time if I don't use the first time. When it comes to using, I avoid the first opportunity, but when it came to my writing, I had to move forward.

While I know how the first book turned out, since I am writing the second one, there were unexpected fears that arose from getting published. Writing and being published for the first time led to consequences I hadn't thought of and couldn't have imagined. I had to revisit my expectations and my level of acceptance surrounding my writing and my hopes of having a writing career. My mom, God love her, was the one who pointed out what caused these new fears. At first I wanted to get mad, but I knew I couldn't. The message came from my mother, and I don't get mad at her; I used to get mad at her, but I do not anymore. I discovered that she was right. She pointed out something I had overlooked. If I wanted to get mad at someone, I needed to get mad at myself for not seeing the truth until she pointed it out to me.

My mother told me that not everyone would love the book. She was talking about the first one, but this pertains to any book—to anything, actually—yet I hadn't consciously thought of it. While this was an easy truth to swallow, she hit me with something else that was more difficult to stomach.

She said that some people would like the idea that I wrote a book; they would support me. Other people would, whether through jealousy or misunderstanding or for some other reason, resent me for writing it, especially about something as subjective as recovery. This hit me very hard. I had signed the contract, we had completed the editing process, and the book had a publication date. It was too late to turn back. I couldn't necessarily recall the process. Yet while my expectations were only to share my experience with others, I discovered that it might help others to recover from addiction. I also discovered that other people might think differently about my expectations. Here I had expectations that I thought were so simple as to not need any acceptance to temper them. Fear swelled in me like a tsunami, threatening to wash me away.

I could do nothing to stop the process. The book was a done deal—it was going to press. I had to find acceptance, and quick. Fear threatened me constantly. I prayed for help, and I think I got it. Yet I am not sure. The first book has been published and I have yet to meet someone who has given me negative feedback, or told me they think I have no business writing a book about recovery. Since the first book has been published, I expect that some people will read it and not like it, and some people may resent me for writing it; and I am sure there are scenarios I can't foresee.

Here is where my acceptance and my willingness to accept will come in handy. Through my acceptance, which has yet to be tested but which I believe to be strong on this subject, I am already beginning to come up with kind, caring responses for those who may have a negative reaction to my first book, or even toward me personally.

My first sponsor told me not to make up my mind about things that haven't happened yet. I consider his comment to be great advice, and I am doing my best not to make any decisions about anything here, but I am using my ability to project myself into the future in order to discover some kind, caring responses to negative reactions that I am almost certain will happen. I am doing this in order that I may be nice to people—even if they are not nice to me or are critical of my work. I am working on my acceptance, and I am working on my willingness to accept.

I am sure there will be situations and scenarios that I cannot yet dream up, and maybe never will. These I must be able to accept as they come. However, if I have some kind responses ready, I am sure I will be better able to weather the storm of any negative reactions that come my way.

My fear of what other people think of my work and of me has led me to this. Fear is a necessary part of the process. It will guide me through as long as I don't let it paralyze me or run the show. As long as I use the fear and don't let it use me, I should be able to handle whatever comes my way because of my first book being published.

In the meantime, working on this book has kept me very busy, but fear remains my constant companion. My friend/foe fear keeps telling me that I will never write another book; that if I do finish this manuscript, it will be turned down; that if it is published, it will not be as helpful to people, or sales will be poor. Fear tells me I have set my expectations too high, that I will never meet them.

I have to admit that this book has been harder to write than my first. Maybe it is because the second book is always harder. Maybe it is because I have set my expectations higher for this work because I have already published a book. Maybe it's just because I really want to share my experience with people in order to help them. I do want to help others, more than anything. I consider it a kind of payback (or pay-forward) because I read a lot of other people's stuff and I listen to people in meetings and elsewhere, and it helps me. Regardless of the reason, this book has been harder to work on, harder to write, and I assume it will be harder to submit even though I already have a publisher.

Maybe I owe that to my mom. Maybe it was her telling me about the negative side of being published that brought up the fear to begin with. However, I can't stop now just because Mom told me the truth. It would be pretty sad if I did. Fear of the truth doesn't help me.

I am doing what I can to prepare for the results of my attempt to publish this book so that I can accept them as they come. And I thank my mom for pointing out something that should probably have been obvious to me all along. It has helped me to reset my expectations and raise my level of acceptance in anticipation of what might happen. I tell fear, when it crops up, that I will not listen to its negativity. I will only allow it to help me. During this process, I have learned an important lesson: *honest, humble expectations are not only possible, but also necessary. They can be changed too, when necessary, to meet new circumstances.*

When I say humble, I don't mean that I need to keep my expectations low; that would be contrary to my experience. I believe it was my low expectations in the past that kept me in my active addiction. I didn't expect that I could recover. I expected that if I did recover, I would be boring and worth less than I was while I was using.

Even after I accepted that I needed to quit using and get into recovery, I kept my expectations low. I heard other people in recovery also say they didn't like to have high expectations, because then they weren't let down when they didn't get what they wanted or hoped for. I couldn't have agreed more. Happiness and recovery seemed to be too much to ask for.

To have an exciting, varied, fun-filled life and to get the things I wanted out of life seemed impossible. Having no or low expectations seemed to fit what I thought recovery would be like before I got into it. I expected life to be boring and dull when I got into recovery, and low expectations fed my belief. After all, just quitting was a huge accomplishment, in my humble opinion. Wasn't that enough to expect? For some time, I thought that it was—at least until I realized that I wasn't comfortable living a boring life. Then I made the wonderful discovery that raising my expectations would push me to test my limits. I also learned something else.

I must keep my ego out of my expectations.

My ego likes to run away with me. I need to make a conscious effort to keep my ego from interfering with or influencing my expectations. My ego can take control and tell me I deserve to have life handed to me on a silver platter. After all, I quit using, didn't I? Shouldn't people give me a break? Shouldn't they see me for who I am and what I have already accomplished? I think I should get a "free pass" in some instances. Am I right? Well, the answer, as much as I hated to admit it in the beginning, is a resounding NO! I remember early in recovery hearing one person tell another person, "It's almost like you want them to think you are somebody just because you quit using. Well, I'm here to tell you, you aren't going to wake up to headlines in the paper that read, Man Kicks Habit, Mows Lawn."

After we had a brief, yet silent, laugh, the reality of the statement rang true. My last accomplishment is just that: it's the last thing I did. The world wanted to know what I would do next, and I needed to start looking to do the next right thing and keep doing it. Getting into recovery was an accomplishment, but it was only the beginning. I have learned that I cannot think myself into right actions. I have to act myself into right thinking.

I began asking myself, "What can I do next?" I can't afford to rest on my laurels. My program tells me that, life tells me that, and I need to get the message. Some days I do; other days I don't do so well. There is good reason for this. It is fear! However, I must keep going. I must keep trying to do the next right thing. Fear wants me to live in the past and the future, not in the present moment. When I live in the future, fear ruins my present. When I live in the past, fear can ruin my present and my future. Living in the past, focusing on my past accomplishments or miseries, doesn't help me in any way, I need to change this bad habit. It threatens more than my serenity and can threaten my recovery. When fear leads me astray and coaxes me to live somewhere other than in the present moment, then I need to ask myself if it is going to help me become a better person. Will it help me do the things I want to do? Will it help me in my recovery? While sometimes it can, the answer is usually no. Still, it can be helpful to remind myself of what I have done.

I remind myself where using took me when the thought of using crosses my mind. I remember where it led me. Then I look at the things I have done since I got into recovery. I can do this very quickly thanks to the speed at which the human brain works. When I have finished, it is time to move on. I don't need to dwell on the mistakes of my past. Unless there is some deeper lesson to for me to learn from visiting the past, I have found it best to leave it alone. I will not argue that revisiting my past cannot help me. There are so many ways that it can. However, I can't afford to be stuck there for too long. My past is a building block for my life of today, and I must use it as such.

Now that I am in recovery, I can use my experience to help others to recover. My list of accomplishments and improvements since I got into recovery keeps growing, and I can have more accomplishments and make even better improvements.

When I was using, I used to say all too often, "One thing led to another and I wound up . . ." You can fill in the blank here with just about anything from passed out to married. Now that I no longer use, I can learn from my successes as well as my failures to build a better future for myself and for others. I can even use that "One thing led to another and I wound up . . ." attitude I used to have to help me today. The difference is that while I was using, I didn't know or didn't keep track of the things that actually happened; today I can list the things that led up to something happening in my life.

Today I have a long list of accomplishments. While listing them here would be an egomaniacal waste of time, I think it is important for me to retrieve this mental list from my head from time to time to remind myself of how far I have come and of how much my foundation in life has grown. I also need to retrieve this list to see just how much I have to work with, and I am surprised to find that I have accumulated a lot of stuff I never had before. Today I have reason to set my expectations high, and I bet you do too.

Right now might be a good time to get out a pen and some paper and write down your own list of accomplishments so you can see your own building blocks. We all have some positives, some good things going for us, even if we cannot immediately recall them from memory. I bet that if you do this exercise, you too will begin to see how they can lay the foundation for building higher expectations for yourself.

I have found another important thing when dealing with my expectations, and that is this: I should set my expectations of myself high while being gentle with others. You'll notice I didn't say letting others off the hook; I said being gentle. There is a big difference.

I do this with acceptance. Today, I set high expectations for others, just as I do for myself, but I also temper them with acceptance, just as I do for myself. The difference is that I raise my level of acceptance of others right off the bat. I do this for many reasons, but the most important reason is to give them some leeway, not only in what happens, but in how they do the things I hope they will do. I do this because I have learned that there are many ways to complete a project.

When I worked on an assembly line, the jobs were broken down into simple steps. They had job descriptions that detailed every step of the procedure. Even I was amazed at the detailed procedures instructing workers how to perform their tasks when I first saw them. "Reach for screw," "Grab screw," "Place screw to screwdriver," and so on. We used to joke about how they should tell us when and how we should scratch our nose.

Even though the instructions took great pains to tell how the job should be performed, no two people did any job exactly the same way. The differences were subtle because the jobs weren't highly detailed (even though the descriptions were); however, there were differences. Everyone adapted the job to suit him- or herself. This logic applies outside the factory and in other areas of my life. It is just like lessons learned in my recovery program that apply to real life. What I learn in the rooms does not do me any good unless I can incorporate it in my life. I am applying these lessons here in order to overcome the fear of my expectations of others. I have come to know that when I am doing a good job and there is a wonderful result the lessons I learned in my recovery let me know that I am succeeding.

When I have a realistic expectation of someone else and I let him or her know what I expect, then I can let that person do his or her part, and I overcome my fear of losing control. I see my fear of losing control as a fear of losing something I think I have even though I never really have it, "it" being control over other people. I am not saying that I lose my fear of losing control, but I do overcome it, because at least for the moment I let others do their part their way.

When I first started doing this, it drove me a little crazy. I thought I knew how things should be done even if someone else was doing them. Fortunately, I had the assembly line background and remembered how everyone did jobs a little differently. I leaned on this knowledge to help me maintain some sanity until I saw the truth. The truth is that other people get things done, too. It seems this idea should have been easier to understand. During my active addiction, the world went on even though I wasn't much of a participant.

By giving other people credit, I lose a little ego, gain a little more humility, and grow spiritually. It is an amazing transformation, but only if I allow it to happen and stay the heck out of the way.

There is one final thing I would like to mention before moving on, and it has to do with being gentle with others. Being gentle does not mean being a doormat. I cannot afford to let people walk all over me. If someone consistently refuses or simply cannot live up to my level of expectation—tempered with acceptance—I need to make a serious decision. That decision has to do with letting that person go. While I am not sure if anyone can fire a friend or lay one off as happens in the workplace, I have severed some friendships because they didn't work for me. This may sound a little crass, but I believe it is necessary for my own growth to make sure I have good, solid friendships.

A friendship based in part on me having to bail someone out all the time is not a healthy relationship for either of us. We all make mistakes, but friendships are a give-and-take proposition. If I am doing all the giving, then I will eventually develop some sort of resentment. Resentment is a luxury I cannot afford. Resentment is based in fear. The healthier choice is to avoid resentment and choose my friendships wisely. Now don't think for a minute I change my friends every few weeks or months or years—because I don't. I am choosier today when picking my friends than I used to be. This is something I had to learn to do, since I had never put much thought into whom I befriended. That is the way I was during my drinking days.

Fear surrounds this whole operation, but overcoming it and letting people leave my life, or telling them face-to-face that I cannot maintain the friendship, has been a real boon to my own growth. I don't spend a lot of time trying to fix other people—unless they want my help and are willing to do the work necessary.

Good, healthy relationships live on a two-way street; today I treat them that way. I do my best to do my part; I do my best to let other people do their part. Since I started looking at things this way, I have discovered something amazing.

Fear comes from my unwillingness to accept life as it is and wishing it were different. When I was in treatment, I learned the difference between admission and acceptance. When I couldn't answer the question posed to me, the girl sitting next to me answered it. She said, "Isn't acceptance when we know the truth and are okay with it?"

What a shocking revelation that was for me. Real acceptance was laid at my feet. All I had to do was reach down, pick it up, and put it to good use. All I had to do was quit wishing that things were different.

Well, it has been a long time in coming, and I still struggle with it at times, but for the most part I have stopped wishing things were different. I shoot for the stars. However, when I see my feet barely leave the ground, I am not afraid to admit that I missed my mark, or at least I am willing to move through the fear; I am not afraid to try again. Who knows, maybe one day I will get there, and if I don't get to the stars, maybe I will at least land on the moon.

## Emotions

Emotions are a big deal. They are puzzling, perplexing phenomena that make me crazy. I can be so wrapped up in my emotions that I lose track of who I am. There are doctors, psychiatrists, psychologists, and therapists who are much more qualified to deal with serious emotional problems than I am. That goes without saying, yet I feel compelled to say it because what I have to say about emotions is going to be very simple. I have learned to deal with my emotions. I keep it simple, and I do this for two reasons.

I keep it simple when it comes to my emotions because I've realized I have a tendency to complicate things, and emotions are complicated enough already. I also keep it simple because I have found that that is what works for me. I have discovered a side effect of keeping it simple that you might call reason number three, and I won't argue with you if you do. Keeping it simple with something as complicated as my emotions helps me keep it simple with other, more complicated things in life. Keeping this in mind, let's delve into my simple plan for dealing with my emotions.

I can start with "My emotions won't kill me." I learned this fact early on in recovery, thanks to my first sponsor. Suffice it to say, I know my emotions won't kill me. Since this is only the beginning, the next obvious questions are "So what?" "What do I do next?" and "What do I do with these feelings?" The emotions might not kill me, but sometimes they make me wish I were dead.

The answer is simple; applying the answer is not so easy. The answer is that I must deal with them (emotions), and the hard part is that I must feel them too. Knowing that they won't kill me sometimes doesn't seem to be enough; I must simply feel them and know that they will pass. All things do pass eventually, and my feelings will, too.

There are times when I want to crawl into a hole and not come out thanks to some emotional overload. When this happens, I go ahead and do it, if I have the time. I crawl into a hole and feel the feelings, deal with the emotions, and remind myself that this too shall pass.

I make a conscious effort to give myself permission to do this.

It seems to help me realize that I can give myself permission to come back out as soon as I am ready to once again deal with the world. In fact, giving myself permission to do what I need to do, when I need to do it, helps me to practice taking care of myself. I begin to listen to my body, my spirit, and my feelings, and when I practice this principle I become better at knowing what I need and when I need it.

In the old days, I used to get drunk at people. I have gotten stoned at people too, but I chose drunk because it is easier on the eye, ear, and brain for this explanation. I can substitute any addiction, alcohol or drugs. Acting out because of emotions can be harmful regardless of the choice of substance or addictive behavior. In the past, if someone made me mad, I would get drunk at him or her. Used in this way, it even sounds like an emotion: "I'm drunk at you." I used to think "drunk" was an emotion, when it really served as a filter or numbing agent for my emotions. Okay, that sounds a little ludicrous—"I'm drunk at you"—but I used to do it nonetheless. I didn't say it out loud because it does sound ludicrous, but I thought and acted it out just the same. I gave it the go-ahead in my mind, and it must have made sense to my fevered, addicted mind on some primitive level.

Today I know what I was really saying back then, which was "I am mad, so I'm going to get drunk at you." Again, substitute any addictive behavior you like here; I have at various points in my past. I could overeat at people, gamble at people, or get stoned at people. You name it. Either I have done it or I can do it at people. Nevertheless, the truth is that I am simply trying to cover up my real feelings and emotions. Drunk is not a real emotion. When I act out I am certainly not dealing with my true emotions, and I'm definitely not doing so in a positive manner. I do not use anymore, but I have to keep on the lookout for other traps I can fall into, other ways to act out. I have had to come up with ways to deal with my emotions in a positive manner. After all, I can't always crawl into a hole until the undesirable ones pass. I have to live life on life's terms, and sometimes this means going out in public when I feel mad or depressed. Life doesn't always give me a free pass when I don't quite feel up to it. What can I do then? Well, let me tell you what I do. Please keep in mind that I just do the best I can each time I don't feel my emotional best. I know I'm a long way from mastering my emotions.

When I feel less than happy, yet life calls me to duty, I do my best to let go of what I am feeling. I do not stuff my feelings. When I stuff my feelings, I tend to want to drown them with alcohol, bury them with food, numb them with narcotics, or throw money at them to make them go away. I don't do these things anymore. Since I now know none of these things work—and are actually a danger to me—I no longer stuff my feelings. What I do instead is put them on hold until I can get back to them. It isn't always easy, but I do the best I can.

I have discovered that this tactic works in degrees or percentages. Sometimes I can get 90 percent happy in order to go out. Other times I may only reach 25 percent happy. I do get at least a little bit happy in order to go out and to deal with other people and the world. I have discovered that if I live in the happy part, if I focus on being happy, my happiness will grow. Twenty-five percent may become 30, 50, or even 75 percent.

The key is to remember that I have not dealt with the emotions I left at home. When I do return, I may find that I am so happy that I don't want to deal with those lousy feelings and emotions. This is a time to get honest with myself. I must determine whether I am getting over them, they are passing on their own, or I am trying to stuff them. If I am able to get brutally honest with myself, I will know the answer.

If I am able to let them go, let them pass, or give them to God, then I can do so and consider myself safe in the process. However, if I have any reservations about how well I have dealt with my emotions, I must revisit them. I must feel them for what they are. I must do this until I know I have done what is necessary to allow the feelings to step into the past and stay there, where they can no longer hurt me, where I can learn from them instead of fight with them.

As I learned to do this and grew in my ability to do it better, I also learned that I could be more careful in how I invested my emotions. I am still learning to watch my emotional investment in others, but I am getting much better at it. While some things I don't have a lot of choice about—I love my family very much, and I am heavily invested there and elsewhere—there are also areas of my life where I can decide whether I want to emotionally invest at all, and if so, how much. I do this by determining how important things are to me. This was a relatively new concept to me when I first entered recovery. I had not given the idea any thought before. It seems that I used to let other people determine how invested I should be in a situation, place, or another person. By giving away my control over this matter, I gave away any chance I had at dealing with my emotions. After all, I was giving my emotions away from the beginning.

I used to invest my emotions haphazardly at best. This haphazard habit of investing my emotions was detrimental to others and me. People and things in which I invest emotionally tug, prod, and pull at me. I now know that I must invest carefully. Today I do my best to pay attention to how I invest myself emotionally.

In recovery, I have learned to "play the tape all the way through" when it comes to my using. I know what happens if I take one drink or drug. When I play the tape all the way through, I can see the end result before I pick up or act out. "Playing the tape" helps me keep from making bad decisions regarding this area of my life.

I can do the same thing with investment of my emotions. I can play the tape all the way through in my head and try to determine if I think it is wise to invest myself emotionally in something before I do it; I look before I leap. Of course, I can't always be sure my prediction is correct. I can't predict the future (not by a long shot), but I can get an idea of whether it might be wise to use caution when it comes to how I make my emotional investments. I have also learned that I don't have to make snap decisions. I can take time to talk to my twelve-step program sponsor and other people I trust before I make these tough choices.

Let's look at an example of how I might be cautious about emotionally investing myself before I leap. I meet new people all the time. Most of them remain acquaintances. I don't make friends easily, partly because I am cautious in this area, and I have a hard enough time maintaining the friendships I already have. There needs to be a good reason to add a new friend to my list. Still, I like having friends, and my natural tendency is to want more of them—my drug of choice has always been more. Whatever I have, I want more of it.

Because of my tendency to want more, I am careful about how quickly I allow myself to add people to my list of friends. I don't hesitate to add them to my acquaintance list; I don't see anything wrong with that, but to add someone to my friends list means I will need to take time out of my already busy life to tend to the new relationship. I know he or she will want me to do things; this person will make demands on my time and add to any guilt I may feel about not doing my best to maintain the relationship.

Before I allow this to happen, I need to make sure I am willing to do my best to follow through and provide them with the things I believe friends should give each other. Therefore, I need to make a conscious, calculated decision on the matter. If I add someone new to my life, I know I will feel guilty if I don't follow through, so I have to be willing to follow through, or I need to keep them off my list of friends. It may sound a little rude, but I don't think it is. After all, if I make a new friend and can't follow through and be a good friend, I have done harm to myself and to the other person. It would be better not to solidify the friendship in the first place. The truth is, if the friendship is meant to be, it will happen naturally over time. I don't need to rush the process. When I try to rush the process, I usually make bad decisions, so I do my best to make a good decision. Then I accept the decision I made without fear and without regret. I also do my best to avoid making decisions or solving problems when I am feeling angry or low, because I have less sense and wisdom available when I am feeling poorly. Making decisions when I am not feeling my best—not necessarily happy, but not mad or sad or feeling guilty, either—has caused me problems in the past. I do my best to avoid these problems now.

My first twelve-step sponsor provided me with a good policy on making decisions. He said, "My rule is, if you have to have an answer right this minute, the answer is no; if you can wait, and let me think about it, I might change my mind."

While I may not say this out loud, I do say it in my head when asked to participate in something. I'm not trying to buy time just to stall. I want the time to think so I can make a good decision, one I can follow through on and that isn't wrapped up in emotion—especially fear, but any negative emotion. After all, the better decisions I make the first time around, the less I have to go back on my word or say, "I'm sorry." I am doing my best today to feel my feelings and to know when my emotions are trying to run the show and to stop them from doing so. I do my best to remember that they won't kill me, to actually feel them, and to let them go when I am through with them, which is usually after I have learned something new. By doing this I have learned to take my feelings and emotions less seriously.

As I practice taking my emotions less seriously, I find there are positive side effects to go along with the practice. By taking my lower moods less seriously, I can avoid most arguments and conflicts. I can do this by not snapping at people I care about for what may seem to them to be no reason at all. Because I create less conflict in my life, there is less fear.

For the most part, I see my emotions as tools; it was not always that way. Like fear, emotions exist to tell me things are off just a bit. If I am paying attention, I can use my feelings to guide me from where I am to where I want to be. This is true even if the feelings themselves cause me to take a short detour.

## Experience

This will be a short section, but let's not allow its brevity to make us think it isn't important. My experience has made for great things in my life. It has helped me to help other people in ways I could never have imagined. I never used to give experience much thought. I do so today because it is more important than I ever imagined.

My experience with addiction has allowed me to help other people recover from an illness that is chronic and terminal. That's nothing to sneeze at, but I am discovering that there is more to experience than meets the eye.

Every decision I make adds to my experience. My experience changes my reality—or, if you prefer, the world as I see it. By participating in life, I change the world through my presence; by withdrawing, I change reality by my absence. Whether I am there or not does make a difference. This has led me to take my decisions about where to go and what to do more seriously. I need to ask myself what I want to participate in; I need to ask what I want to experience before I go out into the world each day. Before I accept an invitation to do something, I need to ask myself if it will be worth my while.

This can be scary, partly because it sounds selfish and almost rude, but I assure you it is not. I have only so many days to live before I leave this world, and I want to make the most of the days I have left. Choosing what I do in a willy-nilly fashion, without much forethought, led me through a world of addiction. As I choose more carefully, I find myself gaining experience that I can use for the betterment not only of myself, but of other people and the world at large. So when I say I need to make sure it will be worth my while, I am including the things I touch in life, all the while remembering that by participating I change the world through my presence, and by withdrawing I change the world by my absence.

Still, for the most part, I gain experience through participation. I must go forth and do things. I must work through my anxieties and apply myself to the world in order to gain more experience, more wisdom. I must do this so that I can help others, help the world, and help myself. These are reason enough to work through any fear I might have of doing or not doing something. However, today I do not allow fear to tell me I can't do something I want to do.

If I choose not to do something, it is usually because I have something else—something I deem more important—that I must do. Other times it may be because I need to "recharge my batteries" through rest and relaxation. I have to remember that I need to take time for myself and avoid spending all my time thinking and doing. Experience is a wonderful teacher. Wisdom comes from experience. Wisdom doesn't come with age. Someone can lie in bed and grow old without gaining any wisdom.

Today I desire wisdom. I want to make smart, solid, informed choices. I want the ability to discern or judge what is true, right, or lasting. I want good judgment.

To get it I must learn from my experiences. To have good, educational experiences, I must look through the fear that tells me I have to do this or I can't do that. Then I need to choose the things I want to do and do them.

What I do matters. It matters to my family and friends, sure, but to the world too. I learned this by looking back at how much of an effect I had on those close to me while I was in the midst of my addiction. The effect was serious, dramatic, and negative. Today I can have the same profound effect on others, but in a positive way. I must look though fear and choose what I want to do while letting my current level of experience guide me in my decision-making process.

When I make a poor choice (or see or hear of someone else making a poor decision), there is more experience to be had and wisdom to be gained. I have heard it said that "good judgment comes from experience; experience comes from bad judgment." I have made enough bad choices to last me the rest of my life. My problem is that I wasn't paying attention to gather the wisdom offered from these lessons when I was in the midst of my active addiction. Today I do my best to learn from all the experiences that come into my life. Whether they are my mistakes or the mistakes of others, I want to learn all I can, and I want this wisdom so I can help other people learn from it, too.

## Ego

Ego is a giant barrier to learning. Let me shorten that. Ego is a giant barrier. When I let ego run my life I don't learn, because I already know everything. I also don't learn because people won't even try to help me since I already know everything.

One time at work, I was supposed to go out to the dock and learn to drive a fork truck. Operating a forklift is pretty much like driving a car, with a few different controls and forks used to pick things up. It was no big deal. However, learning to "work the dock" was another thing altogether. There was a schedule to learn—trucks came and went at certain times. The shipments were always different based upon what we needed. While a truck might be full, our dock would rarely need everything on the truck—it would be visiting other docks as well. We had to know what came off what truck and what went back on which trucks so we could put the empty containers inside the right trucks. The job was complicated for a new guy, yet it was doable.

I started this new job on the dock with another worker. The other worker had driven fork trucks before at another company, and when we hit the dock, he was proud to tell all the guys who would be training us that he knew how to work the dock from his previous experience. I, on the other hand, told them I knew nothing of working the dock and would appreciate any help in learning the job. Guess who got the help. I didn't realize it at first, but the trainers were all working with me. They showed me so much that my head hurt from all the new knowledge I tried to cram into it. I gathered as much of the information as I could and reminded them that I would probably forget a lot of it and need help later. They all gave me a knowing nod of the head.

Halfway through the shift, as I was just beginning to get the knack of what I was doing, I noticed the other new worker was having all kinds of trouble. I asked the dispatcher (dock leader) why the other worker didn't get more help. The dispatcher said, "When he came out here, he told us he knew how to work the dock. You can't teach someone like that. He'll come around, and when he does, he'll ask for help. Until then, we'll have to do our best to cover for his mistakes."

Even though the other new worker had worked a dock before, this dock was so different from his previous experience that he couldn't figure it out on his own. Eventually he did ask for some help.

While I was learning the job from the people who knew how to do it, he was trying to reinvent it or figure it out for himself. In the process he wasted a lot of time—his and the other workers'—and made enemies, or at least got off to a bad start with the veterans on the dock. I learned the job quickly and made new friends in the process.

Now I don't tell this story to boost my own ego because I happened to do things right. Truth is, I had no idea how to work the dock, and I was simply smart enough to tell the truth to those who would be teaching me the process. If I *had* had experience, I probably would have done the same thing the other new worker did, and suffered for it.

I tell this story to show how a little humility can go a long way toward living a happier, more relaxed, easier life. Even if I know how to do something, I can still learn from others who also know how to do it by asking questions instead of showing off my own abilities. If I truly do know a better way than those around me, there will be plenty of time and opportunity to display my talents later. However, if I listen to my ego, I will usually make an ass of myself before I get a chance to find out what it is we are supposed to be doing.

While I can often tell when my ego is trying to run the show, it can sometimes be difficult to know when it is raising its head—or swelling mine. Because of this, I am learning to keep a vigilant watch for those times when my ego is running amok.

One of the more humorous ways I can tell if my ego is getting the upper hand is when I say something silly like "May lightning strike me if I'm lying." It is rather arrogant to think God couldn't hit me if He wanted to. Besides that, a lightning strike is only one of many ways God can teach me, or show me who is really in charge. So having God (or some Higher Power) in my life helps me check my ego more consistently. Checking my ego helps me be more friendly (which is how I make friends) and more teachable.

Since learning helps me gain wisdom, and wisdom helps me live a better life and help other people, I have found learning to be at the core of my new life. I have learned things from some unexpected people, places, and things.

I have realized that it is about the message, not the messenger. I can learn if I am willing to learn. I can learn from others. It doesn't matter if they are smarter than I am or not; I can learn from them. Even if they are not as formally educated, or have less time on a job or project, they may have a better way to work with the current task. They may have a talent that I don't have. Everyone has different talents, so I need to allow others to show me what they know without assuming they are incapable of performing a particular task. I must give them the chance, but I can only do so if I check my ego first.

It is easier to be humble if I remember where I have been. I have made some huge mistakes in my life, and I need to remember that. I can remember that easily if I remember the way I behaved while in my active addiction. After all, only an alcoholic rewards himself for not drinking by taking a drink. I have done that. Remembering that can put my ego in its place.

False pride is a slippery form of ego. To get a hold on it, I need to learn to just say thank you and then shut up. I learned this from a friend who told me that I always said something along the lines of "Oh, I didn't do all that much."

He told me that I was fishing for more compliments by saying such things. Then he gently reminded me that I needed to simply say thank you and then shut up. Since then I have noticed how well this practice works. I have also noticed how hard it is to do. With practice, I am getting better at it and it is getting easier.

I have discovered another way to check my ego. I noticed that people tend to call bad things that happen "an act of God." Hurricanes, floods, or anything that doesn't go their way fits in this category. At the same time, they want to take credit for anything good that happens. I used to do this. As I watched, I noticed other people doing the same thing.

When something good happens, we tend to want credit. I think that's normal. However, today I fight the urge. I see no need to take credit when things go right. If I am truly deserving of credit, my efforts won't go unnoticed. I don't need to take the credit; it will be given to me.

I learned this from my first sponsor. He loved to say, "If you like something I did or said, give credit to God. If you don't, well, that was probably me putting in my two cents' worth."

While I ask myself who should get the credit today, more often than not I keep my dialog internal. It helps me to remember that I am only a part of the whole, a cog on the wheel, a participant.

Chauncey, my first sponsor, was the most humble man I have ever met. He was also the happiest man I have ever met. I tend to believe the two are closely related. And I believe this because, from all I have been able to observe, removing ego removes fear.

The more humble I am, the less I tend to overreact to life. The less I overreact, the more relaxed I am. The more relaxed I am, the easier it is to deal with fear.

# 07 | Time and Worry

Time seems to feed my fear. There aren't enough hours in the day to do everything I need or want to do. Worst of all, I don't get enough sleep, and I am always running behind schedule. Because of the lack of time and sleep, I lived in constant fear—fear of not getting things done, of not being good enough, of letting myself and other people down.

At least that's the way it used to be for me. I have learned to take time a little less seriously over the past few years. Because of this new attitude, I have calmed my life and removed a lot of the fear I used to have about time. It has provided some beneficial side effects as well. I live more in the moment and less in the past and future, I can focus more on what I am doing when I am doing it, and I have less stress.

I used to live in constant fear. I was afraid people would find out about my checkered past, label me a loon, and leave me behind. I also carried a lot of anxiety about the future, the difference being that I wouldn't live up to my hopes and dreams. I have hopes and dreams that I want to live up to now that I'm in recovery, as opposed to the barstool dreams I used to make up to make me look or sound good. I was afraid I wouldn't be good enough—no matter what I tried or accomplished. After all, there weren't enough hours in the day to do everything I wanted to do, or so I thought.

I became so preoccupied with what might happen and what had already happened that I lost sight of what was actually happening. What was actually happening was that my life was slipping away while I was trying to live it in the wrong tenses (past and future). I had to get a grip on time, but I wasn't sure how to do that. Time is slippery.

Time seemed like the tortoise in the Aesop's fable "The Tortoise and the Hare." Time was the tortoise and I was the hare. I would run myself ragged getting ahead, in the process wearing myself to a frazzle. I would then think I had time for a break, only to find time passing me by all too quickly. I repeated this process for most of my life, until I decided that what I was doing was a form of insanity. After all, I was doing the same thing over and over and expecting different results. Something had to change, and I knew time wasn't going to volunteer that change. I set out to change myself. The question became "How can I change to meet time's demands?" I first had to look closely at how I was spending my time. The biggest thing I noticed was that even though I kept saying that I wanted more time, when I received more time I often wasted it. Then I felt guilty for wasting time.

Fear took the opportunity to feed. Wasting time led to guilt, and guilt fed my fear. I couldn't change time, and I wouldn't get more hours in a day. I needed a new attitude.

As I began looking around my life, I realized I was doing (or trying to do) too many things. I was the hare, running and running, only to collapse. My problem wasn't time at all; the problem was how I was using it. I was cramming too many things into my day, then trying to do them all. All the while, my brain screamed at me, "But I need to get all these things done!"

Then I asked myself, "Do I really need to get them all done? Who says so?" Two things my dad told me over the years rang true, followed by one thing my first sponsor told me very early in recovery when I was trying to make up for lost time. I tended to want to make up for years lost to drinking and drugging.

My dad told me, "You can do anything you want to do; you just won't be able to do everything you want to do." He followed this up with "If you died today, do you think the world would stop?"

My sponsor added, "Don't try to get too good by Thursday."

Wherever these sayings may have come from, they rang loud and clear in my head like clanging cymbals, grabbing my attention and making me listen. As I considered these thoughts, I began to get a grip on how I was spending my time.

If I can't do everything I want to do, even though I can do almost anything I want to do, I knew I had to learn to prioritize. Since I'm not insane, just a little crazy sometimes, I knew the world wouldn't stop if I died. This understanding gave me a clearer view of the big picture. The truth is that the stuff I do isn't nearly as important as I give it credit for. Sure, some things are important, but I was treating everything I do as if it were a life-or-death emergency. On top of that, I was trying to make up for lost time (years of lost time), and I was trying to get it all done right this minute. No wonder I was driving myself crazy. I was probably driving others crazy too! The first decision I made had to do with treating things as life-or-death situations. I decided that unless it actually is a life and death situation, I should prioritize. Then I began prioritizing the things I wanted to do. I made a list. When I was finished, I knew I could never get it all done by Thursday.

Then a crazy thought hit me: there's a Thursday every week! My sponsor didn't tell me there was a Thursday every week, and the thought never crossed my mind. I guess it was a good thing that I didn't figure this out, because when I got into recovery I needed to simplify my life, not make it more complicated. Part of simplifying my life was living in the present and not in the future. I had to learn to live life on life's terms, and I didn't need to do everything I wanted to do by Thursday, only what I needed to do. My challenge was figuring out what I needed to do.

At first, my list seemed long because it contained what I wanted to do and what I needed to do. I couldn't possibly do it all. I broke my list down into things that I must do by next Thursday and things that could wait until another Thursday. Then I broke them down further into a daily list. I was less afraid that I could not finish everything I wanted to do, because the daily list made my life more manageable. The most important thing I did when making these daily lists was to put myself first. By putting myself first, I don't mean I became selfish. By putting myself first, I made time for me.

The second most important thing I did was to allow myself time to do the other things on the list. I finally understood that whatever it was I wanted to do, I had to allot time to complete it. Previously, I had difficulty with this part of the process and would get anxious, panic, and lose any control that I thought I had. My fear grew, because I felt as though I had failed when what I had were unrealistic expectations of my ability and resources; time is a resource.

The third most important thing I did was to remove everything from the list that didn't have a deadline. I listed projects like building a new bookcase, cleaning the gutters, or changing the oil in the car. These things got their own separate list, and I got to them when I could. I was amazed to see that some things on this secondary list I never did.

Oh, I changed the oil, cleaned the gutters, and built the bookcase. But there were things on the list that carried little importance to me, where before I was in the habit of assigning life-and-death urgency to everything I wanted to do, like shopping for new clothes, cleaning the basement, and re-landscaping the house. These types of projects dropped off my "must do" list and appeared on my "might do" list. They may be done someday, when they become important, but for now they are where they should be. They are in the "not all that important" pile of things I might get around to when I have time. This has freed up time, and has lessened the amount of guilt I have to carry. That makes my day, every day, a lot easier, and I have less fear.

Another thing I discovered is that every time I say yes to someone, I am really saying no to someone else. This has made it easier to say no to things I don't necessarily want to do—even when the people asking me to do these things are family or close friends.

When I say yes to one thing, I block off that period because I am now busy during that allotted time. In essence, I am saying no to any and all other potential activities that may come along. Now, I'm not saying that I tell people I won't do things just to keep my calendar open for future possibilities. What I am saying is that I keep in mind that there is only so much time available each day, and I need to make sure I use it properly. In the meantime, I am allowing myself time to take care of me, too. Today I consider proper use of my time to be doing the things I want to do or the things I need to do first. If I don't take care of me, I can't be fully there for others when the time comes to do things with or for them. Since I have discovered that I am the kind of person who needs to relax a little to recharge my batteries, I take time to do that, too. I like to take time to sit quietly and let my mind wander and settle upon positive thoughts.

Blaise Pascal once said, "All men's miseries derive from not being able to sit quietly in a room alone." I have learned not only that I can do this, but that

I need to do this if I am to be at my best, while maintaining a necessary level of serenity and freedom from fear.

I used to use because I couldn't stop my brain or slow it down, and it made me uncomfortable. Today I can sit and watch TV without turning it on. I stare at a blank screen and let my mind wander, following it wherever it wants to go, changing its direction when I find it straying off into places I do not want to go. I follow the positive and steer away from the negative unless I need to absolutely, positively deal with the negative. If I must deal with the negative stuff, I deal with it, and then I refocus and center myself in positivity.

One of the strangest things—something I didn't believe possible until I did it—is that taking time to relax, to sit in a quiet room and be quiet, helped me get more done. I used to think the only way to get things done was to run, run, and run. On the contrary, taking time for myself helps me recharge my batteries so that when I get to work I am ready to go. I can approach what I need to do with a positive attitude, which makes all the difference in the world.

While I am sitting quietly, I also realize how unimportant things really are. Some things simply fall off my list while I sit and quietly reflect. It's like magic. I do not necessarily get anything done, but I can check something off my list.

I started out watching the TV without turning it on, but today I lie in bed when I first wake up and stare at the ceiling. I imagine my day. I know what I have to do or what I think I have to do and I visualize myself going through my normal day. I always put a smile on my face in my imaginary day. I find it helps me carry on through the real day once I get out of bed.

I can visually go through my day in a few minutes. That's a pretty good return on my time invested, living a whole day in a few minutes. Each time I do this, I have a plan for my day. I can take the past and the future, put them where they belong, and live in today. I can focus on what needs to be done right now—and I finish things quicker without other distractions getting in the way. Probably the most amazing thing about time is that it is a manufactured concept, yet I became a slave to it. Time controlled my life. I wasn't controlling my time. I now see this as a backward way to look at time, and I am doing something about it. My daily schedule includes short periods to relax, and I don't overbook my day. These breaks and rest periods have become very important to me—more important than running myself ragged trying to keep up with a schedule that I know is unreasonable and overly demanding. Yet I still manage to get many things done. If, at the end of the day, there are still things to do, I decide if I have time to do them, or if I will do them. If not, I let them go until the next day.

Giving myself more time to do things means I am less stressed. This in and of itself is a blessing. When I am less stressed, I treat other people better, am less demanding of others and myself, and tend to be happier. Those benefits are big dividends, and since I started reaping them I have become more and more reluctant to give them up. I expect these benefits; they play an important role in my new way of life.

Only I can choose how much time I really need to do something, and today I do my best to be more realistic about that choice. Most things I do I have done before, and I know how long each task takes. Despite this understanding, I used to allot the bare minimum of time when completing a task. I was always stressed and running late. I lived in fear—unnecessary fear—of being late. Today I allow myself the minimum amount of time I think something will take and I add at least 10 percent. Thirty minutes to get ready to go somewhere becomes at least thirty-three—usually thirty-five— minutes. If I have any doubt, I add more time. I schedule extra minutes, then I use them as needed. If I don't need them, I can relax for a few minutes, take a deep breath, and look over my day so far or check to see what is coming up later, just to make sure I did not miss something.

As I live more calmly, I think better. As I think better, I make better choices and live a better life. As I live a better life, I find less and less room for fear to encroach into my being. Taking control of my time by learning to say no when necessary, by prioritizing things and removing the life-or-death urgency I used to assign to everything, by remembering I am not Superman—and that I can do anything I want, but not everything I want—I can remove a lot of fear from my life.

"If not now, when?" is a wonderful question to ask when I am wondering how to spend my time. I can decide to take time for myself. Now is as good a time as any.

## Worry

I have heard it said that "if you worry, why pray? if you pray, why worry?" and I have heard it said that "every thought is a prayer," which means that if I choose to believe these two things I shouldn't worry, because I am praying constantly. Of course, there can be problems with believing "every thought is a prayer." I know. I used to have trouble with it, until I changed my thinking.

When I was still new to recovery, I heard someone say, "Every thought is a prayer," and the more I thought about it, the more I thought, "If that is true, I am praying an almost constant stream of negativity." When I realized this, fear jumped up and took control, and I have since learned that it is never a good idea to allow fear to run things.

I went to my sponsor for help. He told me that if I was going to believe that every thought is a prayer, then I must learn to think more positively. I must change what I think.

After thinking about it for a couple of days, I decided I did want to believe that every thought is a prayer, that indeed I did believe it. I like believing this because it keeps me in constant contact with God. I figure this is a good thing; because He has constant contact with me anyway, why not go in both directions? I also like to look at my keeping in contact with God as staying in the solution; thinking negatively keeps me in the problem. In this instance, fear is the problem and negativity increases that fear, while incorporating positive thinking reduces that fear.

Practicing this principle also helped keep me conscious about what I was thinking. It helped me remove a lot of the negativity from my thinking because I was more aware of the idea that I was constantly "talking to God" with my thoughts. Since I didn't want to send God a bunch of negativity— because I didn't want it coming back to me—I began watching what I was thinking more closely.

By consciously removing negativity from my thinking, I removed much of the worry in my life. Worry is just another form of negative thinking. Why not get rid of it? While this may sound easier said than done—and I will admit that it takes some serious effort to do so—in the end it is more than worth it. Doing away with worry frees up a lot of space in my head for positive thoughts and ideas. It helps me to cultivate a sense of ease and comfort in my life.

As I practiced eliminating worry and negativity from my thoughts through practicing positive thinking and other methods mentioned in my first book, I began to see that my brain was more relaxed. Since my brain was more relaxed, so was the rest of me. My life became more serene, and I could actually think about things that I wanted. I discovered I could "tell" my brain to think about something, then "forget" about it myself, knowing my brain would report to me when it had an answer.

This took time to learn; taking more time to trust in the process also required effort, but I now know to do it all the time. I do it because I can and because I must. I do it because it makes my life easier and more relaxed. I don't have to be "on top of things" all the time. I can let go.

Relaxation and creativity go together, so it's not surprising that the more fear I have in my life, the less able I am to come up with good ideas; the more

I am able to relax, the better I am at finding better solutions. Even when the solution is simple, like knowing when to ask for help, the more relaxed I am, and the less fear and worry I have in my life, the better I am at doing what is needed. Therefore, I need to overcome fear, worry, and the fear that comes from worry. But how do I do this?

I face my fears head-on to learn to walk through fear; I lessen my worries by changing how I think and by removing negativity from my thought processes as best I can. Then I remember to give myself a break; I am human too, after all, and I am going to make mistakes. When I make a mistake, I allow myself only a brief amount of time to kick myself about it. I want to learn the lesson, but I don't want to focus on the mistake. I want to focus on the positive—the way I will do it next time, or what I learned from the mistake. Cutting myself some slack not only helps me forgive myself and move on, but it helps me learn to forgive other people as well, and this will come in handy when the time comes to let bygones be bygones. I believe the human tendency is to do what is right. I am human; therefore, my tendency is to do what is right. I can relax with this in mind because it means that I do my best to do what is right. However, I can't stop there. I must follow this logic when interacting with other people, giving them the same benefit of the doubt I would give myself if I were in their shoes. I do tend to be more lenient with myself than I am with others. I do this in order to forgive quickly and easily, because this will eliminate a lot of worry from my life.

As I forgive others, I am not bothered with whether or not they have forgiven or need to forgive me. Instead, I concern myself with what I need to do to be a good person. I forgive others while at the same time doing my best to make good choices about how I live my life. In the process, I am eliminating a lot of the worry that likes to take up space in my head. By eliminating worry and the fear that goes along with it, I free up space in my brain so it can do my thinking for me. My brain can then get creative and provide me with wonderful solutions to complicated problems. I can also make more intelligent choices, but only if I allow my brain to do its job and not allow it to be bogged down in worry and fear.

Since every choice is a fork in the road, I must choose wisely. Whatever choice I make, I must then let the other choice go and be done with it. Worrying about what could have been causes more worry and fear, and this worry and fear can clog up the system and cause me to make more bad choices. I don't want to get sucked into a repetitive cycle of worry, fear, and bad decisions. I used to live that way. I didn't like it; I have changed, and I am still changing.

Today, whenever necessary, I forgive others and myself in order to move forward in life. If I or someone else makes a bad decision, it is time to learn a lesson and move on. I try to learn from mistakes other people make as well as my own. I don't have to make a mistake to learn from it. That's a far cry from the way things used to be. There was a time when I made the same mistakes over and over again without learning from them. My progress in this area seems to result from being more relaxed and serene in my attitude toward life. I don't rush things as I used to. I used to think things had to be done right now, or I would wait until the last minute and then slap something together haphazardly. Either way, I usually ended up with an inferior product or decision because I wasn't using my time properly, and the worry and fear began to set in. I was living life in a rush, and the results showed in my work.

By relaxing, I can meet a deadline without too much fuss. Deadlines are a fact of life. They touch nearly everything we do. Everything has to be done by a certain time if it needs to be done at all. Worrying about deadlines is detrimental to my sanity and my growth. It slows my thinking process and makes it even harder to get the ball rolling.

I have found that doing things as soon as I can helps move the process along more smoothly. Procrastination doesn't help me manage my time or lessen my worry. Being proactive can help me to manage my time. Even if all I do is make a conscious effort to "tell my brain" to get to work on the problem, to go think about it and report back, at least I have done something. I have made some progress. Quite often if I do this, it is enough, provided that I am willing to wait and listen to my brain when it reports back.

When my brain reports that I should do something, I usually need to do it. If my brain says, "Call someone for help," I should make the call. If I hear a voice in my head saying I should pick up some tools and get to work, then I probably should. I should because my brain is ready to lead me through the process. If I put it off, I may miss out on an opportunity not only to grow, but to get something done as well.

Getting things done or accomplishing tasks relieves worry and frees up more time.

# 08 | Faith

I am more dependent on electricity than I can imagine, yet I take it almost completely for granted. Using it has become such a habit that I have a hard time breaking it, even when I am forced to.

When the electricity went out a few years ago, I found myself constantly trying to use things that required electricity, only to curse the power company and myself. Since the power outage began during the daytime, I tried to use appliances like the microwave to make some lunch, and I had to put a sign on the refrigerator door handle to remind me not to open it so that things would stay cold as long as possible. As the light of day dwindled and night began, I flipped a light switch without thinking, expecting my lights to come on. As the night went on, I tried to turn on several lights, even though I was lighting the living room with an oil lamp and candles. When I would leave the living room, I would reach for a light switch nearly every time.

When I tired of reading by the dim light of the oil lamp and candles, I thought about watching some TV; when I remembered that the TV wouldn't work, I figured I would play some video games, even though I had just remembered the TV wouldn't work. As I reminded myself that video games required the TV, I thought about surfing the Web or listening to some music on the stereo. I may be leaving a few things out, but the point is that my dependence upon electricity is complete. And so is my faith and my reliance that it will always be there to meet my needs.

When the electricity is flowing, this dependence is a liberating thing. I can do all the things I listed above, and they make my life easier and more fun. For some people, electricity makes life not only easier, but also possible. Take a hospital patient who relies on some machine to keep him or her alive. Without electricity the patient would surely die.

After that power failure, I had to ask myself, exactly when I discovered how willing I was to put so much faith in electricity: Why am I so afraid to put that much faith in God? After all, if my faith in electricity makes my life so much easier, wouldn't my faith in God make my life easier too? It seemed a logical question, so I began looking around.

I noticed that people who have faith in God seemed happier than I was when I began the recovery process. People who went to church on a regular basis and people who attended meetings in recovery seemed to be, on average, happier than I thought myself to be. I decided to put this theory to the test, and I was pleasantly, and not so pleasantly, surprised.

The pleasant surprise came when I realized that God had taken away my desire to use. I had simply asked to have my obsession removed, and it went away. It was that simple, almost like magic. Once I turned it over to God, I was freed of my addiction. As I thought of this, I figured it wouldn't hurt to try giving Him some other parts of my life to manage for me as well. I started small just in case He screwed things up.

It didn't take me long to decide God *did* screw things up. I gave Him my finances, but they didn't get any better. I gave Him my relationships, but they didn't get better either.

When I brought this to the attention of my sponsor, he told me, "God only gives so many freebies. At some point you have to get off your butt and do some work." I exclaimed, "But my dependence on electricity gives me a lot of freedom and I don't do anything for that," then went on to tell him how much easier life was before and after the blackout than during it. He listened to my rant so calmly that I knew I was in trouble. I knew he had an answer and, most likely, an answer I wouldn't like.

"You say you don't do anything for your electricity?"

I stopped to think. I wanted to be sure. Then I answered, "Well, I may have to flip a switch, or push a button on a remote control, but that hardly seems like much."

As I watched the smile grow on his face, my heart sank when he replied, "What happens if you don't pay the electric bill?"

"They turn it off," I said, then added, "but it isn't so hard to write a check."

He replied, "And where does the money come from that keeps the check from bouncing? You have to work for that, don't you?"

My easy way out was vanishing before my eyes. My sponsor was right. If I didn't do the work, I couldn't pay my electric bill. If I didn't pay the bill, they would cut off my power and I would be back in the dark. Still searching, I said, "But the rules for maintaining my electricity are well-defined and easy to understand." Then I asked, "How do I know what my job is with God?"

"Pay attention," he said.

"You're not going to make this easy for me, are you?"

"It's not easy for you to pay attention?" he asked.

"Well," I said, hesitating, "I guess I can pay attention, but how will I know when I know what to do?"

"You will know. God will provide you with the answer if you pay attention. When you ask God for help, it would serve you well to listen for the answer. Remember," he said, looking me squarely in the eye, "prayer is when you talk to God. Meditation is when you listen. You should be in prayer and meditation constantly."

"You are asking an awful lot," I said.

"So are you," he countered.

I looked at my shoes, pondering what he had said, and when I didn't raise my head for a long time, he continued. "Try to think of all the things you get from electricity. I'd bet you couldn't list them all if I gave you a day to do it," he said.

I had to agree. As I raised my head, I nodded. "Probably not," I said.

"The same is true for the things God does for you. The difference is that you couldn't list all of them because you don't even know what they are. You ask and ask, but you never listen. You notice some things because they are so obvious, like recovering from your addiction, that no one could miss that. Not even you. But you don't stop and look for the other things God does for you. When things go your way, what do you think? Do you think you did well? Do you think maybe it is a coincidence?"

He stopped there to let it sink in, then he went on. "It's God. But you aren't giving Him credit because you are too busy taking credit for yourself. If you did that with the power company—if you decided you were the source of your own juice—it wouldn't take long for you to quit paying the bill. They would shut off the power. And you would know the truth."

As our conversation went on, I discovered several things I had been overlooking in my relationship with God. Depending on God frees me, like my dependence on electricity frees me. However, I must still do my share. This dependency was probably my biggest discovery. I decided to do my best to give my life to God and to listen to what He wanted from me in exchange for all the freedom He would give me and had already given me in the form of my recovery.

I decided that day to give God credit for the good things that happen in my life. I decided that there are no coincidences. All things happen according to a plan, one that is so far over my head that I need not worry about trying to figure it out. After all, I don't need to know how electricity works to benefit from it. What makes me think that I need to know how God works to benefit from Him?

One of the last things my sponsor told me on this subject was that God would someday ask me for something and He would expect me to do it. My first thought was of the movie *The Godfather*. When I mentioned this to my sponsor, he laughed and nodded his head. He agreed that he saw it the same way—sort of. He went on to explain that God would not ask me to do something I wasn't able to do, and He would also help me do it if I let Him.

Since that day seemed far off in the future, I decided to try it. Gradually, and incrementally, I began to give God parts of my life.

In the fellowship I attend, there is mention of giving my will and my life over to God. I have heard it said that my will is my thinking and my life is my actions. When I first heard this, I figured that pretty much covered everything. If I gave my thinking and my actions over to God, He would have all there was. I would have nothing left; I would have given it all away.

Yet I saw the results I received when I gave God my addiction. I couldn't *not* try, at least a little. I remembered something from the Bible that had to do with the faith of a mustard seed. While I couldn't remember the saying, or where it was in the Bible, I knew what mustard seeds look like. They are tiny. I began to wonder if "faith of a mustard seed" was too big or too small for me to grasp. I wondered if the idea was too big or the mustard seed too small. I had a hard time getting my mind wrapped around the whole concept. I spent several days trying to think my way through the problem when an idea struck with frightening force. The idea was simple, yet scary. The idea is as follows: you can't take a leap of faith if you are too busy thinking.

Fear stood in my way. It kept me thinking instead of taking the action I needed to take.

I decided to take a leap, to give God something, some part of my life. As soon as I gave it to Him, truly gave it to Him, without reservations, part of my life began to change for the better.

I can't tell you what it was that I gave up first. I don't honestly remember. I know it was something small, probably something almost meaningless, just in case He screwed things up. But this time He didn't screw up, or maybe I should say this time I didn't screw up. I gave it to God and then asked what I needed to do. Then I listened for an answer.

I didn't hear anything. In fact, nothing happened for a while. And even though I don't recall this first time very clearly, I do remember repeating the process many times since. Therefore, my description here comes from many subsequent experiences.

What happened, what continues to happen time and time again, is that I suddenly know what to do.

It might take hours or days or even weeks, but an answer comes, and it almost always comes in the form of knowing what to do, where before I was baffled and had no idea what course to take.

I lived in my addiction for many years. I finally got into recovery at the age of forty-three. My biggest regret was that I lived in my addiction for so much of my life. I didn't want to live with that kind of regret; it was a heavy weight to carry around all those wasted years. I asked God what I could do to be rid of that kind of guilt and regret.

I prayed and I meditated. I talked and I listened. Days went by with nothing. After a couple of weeks, I began to think there was no answer, and that I would have to go through the rest of my life with regret.

One day an idea hit me. It was so contrary to my normal train of thought that it was as though someone else was in my head. The thought that floated in was this: "Why don't you use yourself as an example of what not to do? Why don't you use your experience to help young people in recovery? You can help them get into recovery and stay in recovery by showing what a waste your life had been for so long. In this way, not only will you help others, but your life will no longer be a waste."

Like I said, the idea was revolutionary, or so I thought at the time. I didn't know what to think for sure, but it sounded like a good idea. To this day, I think it took a long time to get the answer because I didn't like the idea of becoming a good example of what not to do. The question then became what to do next. I couldn't simply go around stalking young people and telling them, "Don't be like me and waste your life away chasing addictions." I had an answer, but no possible plan, and no course of action.

As I have learned, when I don't know what to do, I pray. I said something like "Okay, God, if you want me to help young people, if that is how you want me to rid myself of this regret, then you put young people into my life and I will help them." I went on to say that I would need His help in helping them because I was breaking new ground. I was in uncharted territory; I felt clueless. I waited for some sign that He had heard what I said. The answer to my challenge to God came swiftly. Young people began asking me for help. Soon I was sponsoring three people, all of them under twenty-five years old; they came to me looking for help. An idea that seemed so foreign to me turned out to be the answer to my prayers. All I had to do was be open to the idea that God would do a better job of running my life than I would, and then I gave Him the chance. All I had to do was flip the switch and be ready to pay the bill.

Getting ready to pay the bill wasn't easy. In fact, I think it took me a long time to get the answer I needed because my thinking was so contrary to what it needed to be. I kept thinking my past was far too tainted to be of use to anyone, and that nothing good could come from my past. I now believe that it took God a while to prepare me for the answer.

When I asked God how I could get rid of the regret and guilt I felt for living so long in active addiction, I wasn't ready to hear the answer. I could be a good example of what not to do with your life. I still don't like it the way I like a good meal. However, I have come to enjoy the fact that something good has come from all those years. The majority of the people who ask me to sponsor them are under the age of thirty; most of them are even younger, at least when I begin sponsoring them. I enjoy working with and teaching young people.

I'm sure that living in a town that has a college and borders another town with a university helps to give me a fresh supply of young people to work with. I meet many young people in the program, but they still have to ask me to be their sponsor, and that's God doing His part. Another important thing He does is to provide me with ways to help these young people. Occasionally the opportunities He provides surprise me.

I have learned that I need not be squeaky-clean to use my experience as an example. In fact, the impurities of my life are what help me the most.

When I took a chemistry class in college, I learned that ultrapure water does not conduct electricity very well at all. I was shocked (no pun intended) to find that it is the impurities in the water that conduct electricity. This led me to wonder: if I were pure, maybe I would not conduct God. Maybe my impurities bring God into and through my life, and into the lives of others.

This got me wondering about how many impurities one might need in order to be able to be helpful. The answer seems to be that it doesn't matter. I have seen God use people who have been through far worse than I have, and I have seen people who seemed barely scratched by life do wonderful things and help many people.

The trick for me in recovery seems to be that I need to continue working on my personal growth. I must continue to overcome my personal demons in order to help others. As I learn to overcome my own problems and issues, I can help others do the same. I should do my best not to go back to my old way of life or to slide back into my old habits or impurities.

Just as water with no impurities is a poor conductor of electricity, water with too many impurities becomes polluted and unusable. I found recovery at just the right time in my life. I don't think that there is a "wrong time" to find recovery, but for me the timing seemed just right. I have just the right mix of good and bad for God to make good use of me. This is true of everyone in recovery. It's true of everyone who's not in recovery, too. The key for me now is to continue to work my way through my issues, using whatever help I may need, so that I may be ready when God needs to put me to work helping someone else. In other words, I should take care of this delicate balance of impurities to maintain my "humanity" or, as some would say, "my God conductivity." Too many impurities and I will start to fry or become polluted. I don't think I have too much to worry about when it comes to becoming too pure.

Faith and action provide me with a new set of experiences from which to draw. Through taking action and having a little faith, and seeing that it works and how well it works, I can teach others how to get what I have. And I get more by giving away what I already have. That is one of the benefits of life in recovery. Through sharing and teaching, I learn how to do the things I am doing. While the repetition of practicing something is a great way of creating a habit, teaching someone else how to do something new drives the meaning of a lesson home. I believe strongly that this is one of the main reasons that my fellowship says, "We must give it away in order to keep it." Through giving it away, through teaching others, we reinforce the behavior in ourselves. In the process, we reinforce in ourselves the lessons we teach others. We learn and relearn the things we need to know.

I need this kind of learning and relearning because I spent a large percentage of my life misbehaving, or behaving in ways that were contrary to the way I want to behave now. I need to reinforce my new behavior every day, every hour, and every second, if needed. Through new experiences, I discover the new and wonderful way of living I have searched for my entire life.

I heard someone say that the program will not open the gates of heaven to let me in, but it will open the gates of hell to let me out.

I laughed at this because I felt like I knew hell firsthand, and I felt as though the program had opened the gates of hell to let me out. Then I found something that almost sent me right back to hell: I couldn't forgive myself.

Forgiving ourselves can be more difficult than forgiving someone else. I think this is true, because I don't feel I am worthy of forgiving myself. Forgiveness must come from a power greater than myself, from God, if possible.

This created a "catch-22" for me. I wanted to forgive myself, but I was afraid that I didn't hold the authority to do so. I believed that only God could forgive me for the things I had done. My fear held me captive in my regret for such a long time, but I finally found relief and forgiveness.

I did it through faith that God would forgive me only if I was willing to be forgiven. To show I was willing, I needed to be willing to do whatever God decided I needed to do in order to make the process work. For me, the answer was turning my past to good use by making myself a good example of *what not to do with your life*. I had to humble myself to make this happen, but I wanted the freedom that I knew would come with it.

Fear stood in the way, but I walked through it—again—and this time I found God waiting to take me on a ride that I still find incredible. The ride keeps getting better every day.

# 09 | Happiness

Happiness is a choice; fear is not. Regardless of what is going on in my life, I can choose to be happy. However, I must want it badly enough. When fear worms its way into my being, I am stuck with it. Oh sure, I can deny it or try to convince myself and others that I'm not afraid, but the truth is that I'm scared.

While I can replace sadness with happiness with a little work, I can't replace fear with another feeling or emotion. The only way to remove the fear is to face it head-on, look it in the eye, and move through it. Well, that is not entirely true; there is one thing that will remove fear, but we will get to that a little later. For now, I want to focus on how I create my own fear instead of creating happiness. After all, if I am busy creating happiness, I can steer myself away from much of my fear-filled time. I say this because I have found that I actually create much of my own fear. There is a saying that goes "I have lived a life of many troubles, most of which have never happened." This is something I do in my head. I create many if not most of my own troubles and fears.

When I spend time thinking about what I don't have and not on what I do have, I create a covetous attitude that defeats my happiness and causes fear. I'm not talking strictly about material things here, either. I'm talking about every aspect of life—family, friends, work buddies, acquaintances, getting enough exercise and sleep, and a full belly. When I am more concerned with what I lack instead of living in the fullness of the life I have, I create my own fears and anxieties. I could never possess everything there is to have in this world. No matter how much money I had or how many people I knew, I would always be a few dollars and a few people short of everyone and everything. There would always be something eluding me, something to dwell on, or something missing. For this reason alone, it makes sense to avoid focusing on what I lack by living in the fullness that is my current situation. Counting the things I have takes my mind off the things I don't have.

It helps to write these things down. I know many people who make a "gratitude list" every day, usually in the morning to start the day off right. When I am grateful I tend to be happy, and when I'm happy I tend to keep fear from encroaching on my life. In this way I can contain my fear by living in happiness and gratitude, and stay lighthearted.

Being lighthearted helps me avoid defensiveness and arguments. I can take a joke and keep my expectations in check. I can laugh at myself for my mistakes and for being human. It keeps me from trying too hard. I don't mean doing my best; I should always do my best. I mean trying too hard or trying to be perfect. Being lighthearted about my abilities helps me remember that I can't be perfect. This too can reduce my anxiety level, because I remind myself not to try to be too good.

Being first, or best, is too stressful, and it doesn't last. All records are eventually broken, anyway. Seldom does a marathon runner who starts in first place cross the finish line in first place. My journey through life is like running a marathon. If I want to do well I need consistent effort and progress rather than trying to stay in first place. While I won't argue that being first or best is always bad, someone has to be first and someone is always best. What I am saying is that I shouldn't drive myself to try to stay constantly at the top. It requires more effort than it's worth. I am constantly looking for the next person who might knock me off my perch. I have to look over my shoulder all the time, and that makes it hard to see where I'm going. I inevitably run into fear and anxiety when I am not watching where I'm going. Like a marathon runner, being second or second-best (or staying in the middle of the pack) isn't bad, and is far less stressful.

When I am looking for something to be perfect, I am automatically unhappy. When I am trying to be perfect, it can drive me crazy with the stress of trying too hard. Perfection and happiness oppose each other. Perfectionism drives me away from happiness. Happiness drives me away from perfection and fear.

I must learn to change the way I think about life and what it's all about. Happiness can keep fear at bay most of the time. It can help me to remain lighthearted. It can help me change my mind. I can mold my mind and change it from a fear-based machine to a creator of a relaxed, carefree way of life through happiness. I won't be bothered as much, and I will allow for mistakes. I will adjust my expectations with acceptance of the way things are.

When I accept things as they are instead of trying to realize unrealistic expectations, I can relax and keep fear where it belongs. As I change my mind from fear to happiness, I can find the only real cure for fear. That cure is love. Love conquers fear. I have found it to be true. In fact, I believe that there are really only two base emotions, love and fear. The remaining emotions always seem to stem from love or fear.

I have also learned to deal with my particular fears—I can love them away. How do I do this? I hope I can answer that question. First, I know there are people smarter than I am who have done scientific research on this subject. I also know that we like to think that we are very complex beings, that we have the ability and the tendency to feel and display many separate and distinct emotions. However, even the scientists who have extensively researched the subject conclude that we have far fewer base emotions than one might think. For example:

- Robert Plutchik, in *Emotion: Theory, Research, and Experience Volume I*,[1] came up with eight—acceptance, anger, anticipation, disgust, joy, fear, sadness, and surprise.
- Carroll E. Izard, in *Human Emotions*,[2] listed ten—anger, contempt, disgust, distress, fear, guilt, interest, joy, shame, surprise.
- John B. Watson, in *Behavioralism*,[3] gave only three—fear, love, and rage.
- Bernard Weiner and Sandra Graham, in "An Attributional Approach to Emotional Development," *Emotions, Cognition, and Behavior*,[4] boiled it down to happiness and sadness.

My two basic emotions come from my own experience, not from scientific research, but it works for me, and maybe it can work for you, or at least help you gather a new insight into how your emotions work on you or can work for you.

To begin looking at my example of love and fear, I refer to the five states of grieving. These are most often described as:

- Denial
- Anger
- Bargaining
- Depression
- Acceptance

While I will allow myself to go through these stages when I experience grief, I still see them as five stages of my two primary emotions.

*Denial* is a refusal to grant the truth of a statement or allegation. I see denial as a form of fear, fear of losing the thing I have already lost or will eventually lose. *Anger* is a continuation of fear carried out in a different form. *Bargaining* is wishing we could get back that which was lost and the fear that we will never have it back. *Depression* is the deepest form of fear because we begin to understand we will never get it back. *Acceptance* is love: we begin to realize that we will never lose the love we had for the person, place, or thing we have lost.

It is at this point that I can begin to move back into happiness. Gradually, depending on how great the loss, I can reach the level of happiness I enjoyed before the loss, despite the nagging fears of denial, anger, bargaining, and depression that might want to remain. Love conquers fear.

This scenario works for me, and it can work with other fears. While fear can be the result of anxiety, nervousness, tenseness, uneasiness, apprehension, worry, distress, and/or dread, I tend to lump the remaining negative emotions in with it. I add to this list loneliness, defeat, guilt, shame, sadness, jealousy, resentment, annoyance, even grumpiness. I do so because I believe that fear is at the root of them all. As discussed in Chapter One, fear is losing something I want to keep or not getting something I desperately want.

When I am lonely, I want company; instead of defeat, I want victory; when I feel guilt or shame, I want blamelessness or innocence. When I think I can't have these things, I feel fear, and I feel fear until I realize that I will, at some point in the future, find these positive traits again. Love shows me the way.

I'm not talking about the kind of love one feels for family or friends. I'm talking about love in the sense that I know, deep down, that things will be okay. I'm talking about unconditional love for myself. When I first learned to give unconditional love, I was shocked at how it felt. In fact, it took me three days to realize that I had given my love to another person without conditions.

I was shocked for two reasons. The first reason was that I had never done it before, at least not to the extent I had this time, and the second was that it felt so good. I felt so good for three days for no particular reason, and it led me to do some soul-searching. Only then did I realize I had given my true, unconditional love to another person. I wanted to try an experiment on myself with this new unconditional love. I decided to try something new, but it took some time. I went several months before I tied it all together, but when I did, the experiment became a quick reality.

I decided to love myself unconditionally to the best of my ability. This was not easy to do. My emotions kept getting in the way, and for a while I thought I would fail. Fear jumped at the chance to put me down, but I resisted.

I came up with my "one swift kick in the butt" rule, which means that I am allowed one swift kick in the butt when I make a mistake. It does not matter how big or small the mistake. Once I have kicked myself, I do my best to learn the lesson; then I move on to loving myself.

I based this whole idea on the fact that if I were to love only one person in the whole wide world, it should be me. I had heard that I must learn to love myself before I could expect others to love me, so it made sense to start giving myself some love—intentionally, consciously, consistently, and unconditionally.

I know this might sound a bit corny, but I told myself several times a day, several times an hour at first, that I loved me; I said it until the habit stuck and I began to feel like I loved myself. When I made a mistake, I gave myself "one swift kick in the butt," then I began loving myself again. I love myself just as I am. After all, if I am to love myself unconditionally, I must love my faults, too. One of the first things that happened was that I had to learn to admit when I was wrong. Then I had to learn to laugh at myself, because laughing at myself is much more fun than kicking myself in the butt. In the process, I had to change my understanding of what caring means. Today I see caring as a concern for my well-being. I can't try to cover up my mistakes and still be happy. The cover-up makes me a mental and emotional wreck. I can't go around kicking my own butt over every mistake, especially the small ones. After all, most mistakes are small, aren't they? I had to start giving myself a break, stop being my own worst enemy, and start loving myself.

Some of the earliest results I began to see, as I consistently loved myself unconditionally, were the ability to laugh at myself and to stop kicking myself. These early results helped me to begin carrying around some self-esteem; self-esteem had been sorely lacking in my life. From this increase in self-esteem came happiness—true happiness, pleasure, satisfaction, and joy. As a result, my life became more than tolerable, it became more enjoyable, and even delightful at times. Today life is more delightful than not, and I can remember a time in my life when I thought that was impossible.

However, to reach this state, I had to do something serious. I had to begin earning what I wanted from life. I had to quit looking for the quick fix or instant gratification. There are no quick fixes for long-term bad habits. My first sponsor taught me this.

I remember one time, early in my recovery, we were talking and I asked him how long it would be before I felt better, now that I was working a program.

"How long did you drink and drug?" he asked.

"Twenty-five years, give or take," I replied.

"Then give recovery twenty-five years and see how you're doing then."

"No way, man. That's too long."

"Oh, it won't take that long, but you should be willing to work at it that long. Old habits die hard, and you will be changing more than just your habit. You will be changing your whole life."

I scratched my head on that one. I thought about it for a while, and after a month or so I brought up the subject again. His answer hadn't changed, but my attitude had. I said, "I've thought about what you said, and I'm willing to give it a shot. I don't know if I have twenty-five years, but I will put myself into this whole-heartedly."

"If you will give it your all, it won't take anywhere near twenty-five years," he told me. Then he added, for emphasis, "Just don't try to get too good by Thursday."

I asked what he meant by that.

He replied, "Stop expecting results. Just do the work."

He had just laid out the definition of unconditional for me.

Today, I can be unconditionally happy. I can use my unconditional love for myself to alleviate my fears, especially my fear of what other people think of me. I don't have to rely on other people for my love or happiness. I give it to myself.

Two other things that like to get in the way of my happiness are loneliness and boredom. I spend a lot of time alone—it is one of the things writers do—but I am rarely, if ever, lonely. I used to confuse the two. I once thought that being alone meant that I was lonely. Today I know that loneliness is wishing I were with others whether I am or not.

When I was in the midst of my disease, I could be lonely in a room full of people. It seemed that I always wanted to be somewhere else, with someone else. I was always going to be happy when . . . If I was at home, I was going to be happy when I got to the party. Once I was at the party, I was going to be happy when I got home. I was never happy in the moment, which is where I find happiness. Happiness isn't in the future; it is now. However, if I am going to be happy, I am trying to live in the future and thus I bring loneliness to my present. I become discontented with the way things are right now—and suddenly I feel lonely, no matter where I am or who I'm with.

The dictionary defines lonely as follows: "without companions; unhappy as a result of being without the companionship of others." I know I can be lonely even in a room full of friends. I can do this by simply allowing my mind to tell me things that aren't true, such as they don't really care about me or I will be happy when (pick any time in the future). If I am not being happy now, I can slip into loneliness.

On the other hand, even if I am at home alone, I don't have to feel lonely. I can choose to be happy instead, and I can do this simply by knowing that I have friends and family who love me and will show that love to me when I see them again. This is a form of delayed gratification—something sorely missing from my life while I was in the middle of my addiction—and I can learn to master this with repetition. I can repeatedly remind myself of the truth: that people love me and I will see their love later, even though I have it now.

After all, I shouldn't have to see their love to know I have it. I don't have to see my car to know I own one. I simply know I own a car and I visit it when I can, or when I have to go somewhere that requires driving. The rest of the time, my car is a long way from my thoughts.

The most amazing thing about loneliness is that if I think of a friend, I can probably get in touch with him if I want to. With cell phones, email, and the myriad ways we have of communicating these days, I can usually find a friend or two if I want to badly enough. Still, the goal for me is to not need to. I should be able to spend time alone and not be lonely. I can do this with a little delayed gratification. But it's easier to do once I am comfortable hanging out with myself, and it is more comfortable hanging out with myself when I am a happy, fun person, not a bored, covetous being always looking for the next big drama. Always looking for something big, or even some kind of chaos, brings me back to boredom, if not loneliness, and boredom is not healthy either. Fortunately, I can overcome boredom. Maybe not at first—

few things are overcome without some work—but with a little practice, I can turn boredom into contentment or even happiness.

I have found boredom to be a man-made notion. It forms from an addiction to excitement and action, whether real or imagined. Boredom tells me I should be *doing* something. In fact, boredom tells me I should be doing something else even when I am happy doing what I am currently doing. It comes from living somewhere, or sometime, other than in the present moment.

I now believe that any boredom I experience today comes from living in lack—looking at what I lack instead of what I have. As was discussed earlier, when I live in lack I find fear. My addiction always told me that I needed to be doing something else, regardless of how much fun I was having at the moment, or it told me that I could enhance the fun I was having if I did something even more fun.

Looking back over my life, I see times when I was bored even when I was with people I liked, doing something I enjoyed. Today I see boredom for what it is—a tool. Today I use boredom to remind me that I have left the present. If I am bored, I am either in the future, dreaming of something more exciting that I would rather be doing, or I am reliving some moment in my past that I think was more fun than what I am doing right now. This can happen anytime, no matter what I am doing, but it seems to happen most often when I am doing nothing or when I am sedentary.

For a large part of my life, I thought doing nothing was the enemy. I thought I should avoid doing nothing. Today I enjoy doing nothing. It is freeing to sit and to do nothing, think nothing, or feel nothing. There are no worries in nothing, and when I have no worries, it is easy to be happy. I simply allow myself to enjoy the time of nothingness. I relax into the idea that doing nothing can actually be productive.

When I leave the state of nothingness, when I become active again, I am more relaxed and able to wear life more loosely. I don't take things so seriously.

I usually have better ideas about what I would really like to do. Instead of running or jumping from one thing to another, searching frantically for that which will make me happy—even if I realize the happiness will only be fleeting—I generally leave a state of doing nothing with an idea, or even a realization that I have found something I want to pour myself into.

I began enjoying doing nothing by watching TV. I did this by not turning the TV on. The first time it happened by accident. I found myself staring at a blank TV screen, not knowing what to do next. When I realized that I was staring at a blank TV, I did a quick check to see if I had lost my mind. A television, after all, is made for watching when it is turned on, and I certainly wasn't doing that. As I checked myself, I realized I hadn't been doing anything at all, really. I was sitting in my chair staring at the screen; I wasn't thinking, dreaming, or pondering anything of importance.

As I checked further, I realized that I hadn't been bored or lonely or unhappy, either. I was simply relaxed, composed, and content. As I came back to myself, I realized that I wanted to do something, and I knew exactly what it was I wanted to do. It wasn't very exciting, something like going to mow the lawn, but I had something that I really wanted to do—not something manufactured by frantically searching or something dictated by society, but a genuine desire to do something.

It was from this first realization that doing nothing could be beneficial that I began watching a blank TV screen. I stared at the blank screen more often and for longer periods, and nearly every time I did, I came away from the experience with an idea to do something that was real. It was also something that I needed to do, not something that seemed like a good idea at the time. The idea wasn't always a chore such as mowing the lawn; sometimes it was making a purchase—buying something for myself or for someone I care for deeply. Other times the idea was a better way to go about something I do often, or a way to do it more efficiently or effectively.

What I do with my solitary time or the ideas I come up with doesn't really matter. What matters is that I take the time to do it, and the results are positive. I am not bored or lonely. I just am. When the time has passed, I am happy, calm, and ready to move on to the next challenge in life. I have discovered that "recharging my batteries" is a necessity for me today; as with many things I do in my life, I need to recharge myself. If I drive my car without refilling the gas tank, I will run out of gas. If I don't change the batteries in my small electrical gadgets, they will stop working. The same is true for me. If I don't take time to recharge, I will stop working properly. While sleep is a form of recharging, I need to take time while I am awake to allow my mind to work or to wander. I have found two productive ways to do this. I consider them both to be forms of meditation for me.

First, there is letting my mind do what it wants to do, where I focus on nothing in particular. Second, I set my mind on an idea that I want to work on (my writing, or something I need to work out) and watch to see what happens as I let my mind relax on the subject.

In the first instance, I usually find a passion—something I want to do or learn. In the second instance, I am visualizing my idea coming to life. Once I find my passion, desire, or something I simply want to do, I visualize it happening. Athletes and performers use this technique, and it seems to work well for them. Once I visualize it in my mind, I go work for it. Doing the work is what really makes things happen. However, while I am spending time "doing nothing," I am preparing, and preparation is important.

Much more of life is preparation than I used to believe, or even think possible, let alone necessary. I make a list before I go grocery shopping; I make reservations before I take a trip; I pack bags and prepare the car for the drive or buy plane tickets; in fact, before I leave the house, I clean up. These tasks are all part of preparation before I tackle the real tasks I wish to accomplish.

I have come to see preparation as such a large part of life that I need to enjoy it. It's part of the process, too. I prepare, I act, and I see the results. Generally speaking, the better I prepare, the easier it is to act, and the better the results. Preparation was simple, yet difficult to do in the beginning.

I can remember the first few times I told people I sponsored that I learned a form of meditation by watching TV without turning it on. I am sure they thought I was crazy at first, but a few of them have tried it and they tell me it works for them too. Some of those I have sponsored have continued to practice traditional forms of meditation. I have as well, and I can tell you that my experience with meditation has been far better than I ever imagined possible.

I used to think it was crazy to spend time doing nothing. You don't get anything done doing nothing, I thought. It had to be crazy. I have learned something from this, too. I have learned that not everything that sounds crazy is crazy. This fresh perspective has helped me with two life challenges. One is keeping a more open mind; the other is caring less about what other people think of me.

I tend to keep a more open mind about what other people do, or tell me they do, that works for them, no matter how wild the idea; I do this because if I don't give it a try, I will never know if it will work for me.

On the other hand, I don't cringe or fill with fear if someone tells me that my ideas sound a bit crazy. I know they work for me. Why should I worry about someone who has never tried it telling me it won't work? As I practiced this new way of thinking about what other people thought, an interesting thing happened.

At some point, I stopped caring what others thought, cared about, or needed. I only cared about what I thought when it came to me. Others can think, care about, or need whatever they want. Their thoughts, cares, and needs don't and won't affect me. If they do, I can act (or react) as needed.

However, for the most part I can let them think and do as they see fit. They don't need to think or act like me. They certainly don't need to like me for me to like myself.

What other people think of me doesn't define me unless I let it. What I think of me—and even more, what I do—defines the real me. For this reason, I do the best I can. I share what I have to the best of my ability. I let other people take what they think they can use, and throw the rest away. It's what I do. It helps me to be happy to let other people be what they want to be, whether they want to be happy or not. It is up to them and not up to me. I cannot control them. I can only offer my experience, guidance, and suggested approaches to life and hope they will find something in there that works for them. In the meantime, I need to remember that everyone is doing the best he or she can.

I think we are all doing the best we can with what we have to work with at any given moment. We make decisions, prepare, and act with the best of intentions and with all, or at least most, of our ability. Many people don't live up to my expectations, but maybe that is because my expectations are too high for them at that moment. Instead of getting mad—which ruins my happiness and can even bring fear into the moment—I can give them the benefit of the doubt. I can do this by reminding myself that they are doing the best they can with what they have to work with at the current moment. By doing this I lessen my anguish and I give other people the room they need to live their lives. If I decide that I don't want to be around them because they constantly come up short, I can do that. I can even decide that I don't want to be around them because they constantly outperform me, but I rarely do that anymore. Instead, I stick around to see what I can learn from them.

Being around people who outperform me makes me work harder. I must prepare better and work smarter to achieve the goal, and sharing my life with people who can do things I can't do as well makes life easier for me. If I pay attention, I can become one of those people. I do not have all the answers, and I never did. However, if I remain teachable, my life continues to improve. One of the main reasons I do my best not to decide that I don't want to be around someone because he or she constantly comes up short is that he or she may be looking to me for ways to improve. I have sponsored enough people to see that we all need help from time to time. I have also learned enough from the people I have sponsored to know that I can learn from people I might at first think are not as good as I am. Heck, I have even seen people who I thought had less talent than I have at a task learn, practice, and become better than I am at performing it. If I am smart enough to stick around to help them learn what they need, I will benefit when they show me their method, which is by now better than mine. It's all part of the unconditional love that I must put to work for me. I have to give the unconditional love to others before they give the new and improved version back to me. I get more by giving it away, and I learn in the process.

When I live in love, I can give of myself freely and without worry about the results, like my sponsor told me to do, and then learn from whatever happens. I can help others become better while becoming better myself. You can't help someone climb to the top of the mountain without reaching the summit yourself. Love conquers fear. Happiness keeps it at bay. Yet fear will still creep back into my life at times. It's all part of the process.

My goal today is to be as happy as I can, as often as I can, and do the best I can, and let others do the same. After all, it's only fair; but more importantly, it's fun! Happiness is not what I used to think it was. I used to think being happy meant that I was laughing or joking, or at least smiling. Today I know better, and the dictionary backs me up on this. The two definitions I most often use have little or nothing to do with joking, laughing, or smiling. The definitions state that being happy means being especially well-adapted or cheerful or willing. Some of the synonyms for happy include glad, joyful, and content. Today, when I am content, I know I'm happy, and I know I am living in the moment, which is where I actually live whether I am there or not.

## Chapter Nine Notes

1. Robert Plutchik, "A general psycho-evolutionary theory of emotion." *Emotion: Theory, Research, and Experience, Volume 1*: Theories of Emotion (New York: Academic Press, 1980), 3–33.

2. Carroll E. Izard, *Human Emotions* (New York: Plenum Press, 1977).

3. John B. Watson, *Behaviorism* (Chicago: University of Chicago Press, 1930).

4. Carroll Izard, Jerome Kagan, Robert B. Zajonc. *Emotions, Cognition, and Behavior*, (New York: Cambridge University Press, 1984), 167-191.

# 10 | Patience, Practice, Problems, and Principles

I have heard it said that "patience is knowing how to push someone's buttons, but resisting the temptation," and while that may be kind of funny, it's funny because it's true, at least to some extent. In my using days I had the patience of a runaway train, or maybe I should say of the proverbial bull in a china shop, because a train at least has a sense of direction; I didn't. I pushed buttons because they were there and I knew how to push them. I lived in fear that someone else would push my buttons. What a horrible, vicious cycle to live in.

I have changed my ways, of course, and today I do my best *not* to push people's buttons. Even if they push mine first, I do my best to let it go and not try to get even. The serenity I reap from this practice is amazing. I don't constantly watch over my shoulder to see who is out to get me. Because I am not out to get anyone—that generally means no one is out to get me—I can go about my life and let others do the same. In the meantime, I can work on my patience in other ways. There are many areas of my life that require patience. The cool thing is that the better I get at applying patience in one area, the better able I am able to use it in other areas.

After I learned not to go around haphazardly pushing people's buttons, I began to look at life differently when it comes to patience. Since I wasn't so busy looking over my shoulder, I could take the time necessary to look elsewhere. When it came to patience, I discovered that my lack of patience, for the most part, was rooted in fear. I thought that if I didn't get what I wanted immediately, I would never get it. I was afraid that if I lost something, I would never get it back. What a horrible, irritating way to live. I needed to find a different outlook on life.

I had a conversation with my sponsor that rescued me from myself. After the proverbial "Be careful what you pray for; you just might get it" part of our conversation had passed, I asked him how I could learn to be more patient.

"With other people or with yourself?" he asked.

Wanting it all—right now—I said, "Both."

He laughed and said, "You can have both, but it takes a lot of work, and a lot of time."

I sighed, looked at the floor, and said, "That figures. Patience takes time."

"And work," he reminded me.

I wanted to learn to be patient, so I said, "Tell me what to do."

He went on to retell the story of how he had said no to a man wanting to pave his driveway. My sponsor's philosophy at the time was that if the man had to have an immediate answer, the answer would be no. If my sponsor had time to think about it, he might change his mind. He then went on to tell me that I could apply that same philosophy to myself. When I thought I wanted something, if I thought I had to have it right now, the answer should be no. I needed to learn to put things off. I had to relearn how to delay gratification.

"Instant gratification is the enemy of patience," he said. He went on to add that there are several other problems with instant gratification. We get ourselves into all kinds of trouble by following our instincts without thinking things through. He told me to think about what he said and that we could discuss it again later.

"So this is my first lesson in patience, then," I said.

He continued, "In a sense it is, I suppose, but you have to understand that it is also a life lesson. All things take time. That is why I keep telling you not to try to get too good by Thursday. We simply can't have everything we want—especially right this minute, or even in a week. Some things take a very long time and we must do a lot of work to get them. Go ponder this, and we will talk more later."

Learning patience became an itch in my brain that I couldn't scratch. I thought about it a lot, and I kept circling back to saying no. How, I wondered, would saying no teach me patience? Delaying gratification seemed the obvious answer, and I wanted something more to give my sponsor when we next talked about the matter, so I spent more time thinking about it.

Then I heard someone in a meeting say that he had stopped looking for gratification and started looking for gratitude. Something in the way he said it and the way he acted made me take heed of the message. My ears perked up and I listened closely to the rest of what he had to say. While I can't remember what exactly was said, the lesson seemed to be that if I live in gratitude, I will have more patience. Maybe that isn't what he was trying to convey at all. Maybe that is what I heard because I was focused on getting some patience in my life. It doesn't matter to me now because I got a grip, albeit a tenuous one, on something I could do to increase the level of patience in my life. I figured if I was grateful for what I had, then I wouldn't be so inclined to want more—or something else—to "make me feel better." I brought the subject up again with my sponsor and told him what I thought: that if I learned to be happy with the things I had in my life, I wouldn't be so inclined to want other things. I wouldn't always be looking for the next thing to make me happy.

"That's part of it," he said, "and it only applies to you, not other people, but it's a start. Think on it some more."

I looked at him and was about to object. I thought I had done a lot of work and wanted him to give me answers, but the look on his face told me it would be better to forget my objection. I could tell he was set in his way of teaching me patience, that he wouldn't simply *give* me the answer, or answers, I was looking for. As I swallowed my objection, I realized that my having to work it out was part of the lesson. I nodded my head and said I would give it some more thought.

*Delayed gratification is an important form of patience* is the thought that rang through my head for the next week or two. I prayed about it every day, and one morning I woke up with an idea. I decided that from now on, I would not buy anything I thought I needed, unless it was required to live (like groceries), for at least three days.

I made a list of things I thought I needed and kept it handy, adding to it as I thought of items I deemed important enough to add to the list. More importantly, before I went shopping, I made a list of things that I needed and only bought what was on the list. If I saw something I thought I needed, but it wasn't on my list of things to buy, I only allowed myself to make a note of it. Then I left it on the shelf.

Over the years, I am sure this has saved me a lot of money, but it also has helped me learn patience. In turning instant gratification into delayed potential for gratification, I have learned that I don't need to have something—anything—just because I think I do.

Of course, there are exceptions to every rule. Sometimes I need a wrench to finish a job and I must go get it before the store closes, or my computer breaks and I must fix it right away (I do my writing on my computer), so sometimes the three-day waiting period gets waived. For the most part, though, I still stick to this three-day waiting period. I have even modified it so that the more something costs, the longer I wait.

The most amazing thing about the list is that it shrinks as fast as it grows. There never seems to be more than a handful of items on it anymore. It's funny how after three days I find that I don't really want or need most things, so I scratch them off the list.

I hadn't brought up the subject of patience with my sponsor for quite some time, but when I did, it was to tell him what I was doing. My usual mode of operation with him was to tell him what I thought and ask for his guidance. This time, however, he was guiding me to look for my own answers, so I went to him with what I had so far.

He told me that I was doing well. "You started working on yourself first," he said. "That's the right place to start."

Scratching my head, I asked, "Will this transfer to being patient with other people?"

I knew his answer before it left his lips. "Think about it" was all he said.

I nodded and smiled, and he smiled back at me. I was learning.

Since making a list of items that I wanted to buy worked so well, I decided to make a list of chores I wanted to do. Chores such as mowing the lawn, cleaning the basement, washing the car, or replacing the water heater made the list. As usual, I went crazy in the beginning, putting everything on the list. I wrote down the meeting I would attend that day, filling the car with gas, things that didn't need to be on a "to do" list. The list soon became burdensome. It was too big and took too much of my time to maintain. I spent far too much time finding the list, adding to it, scratching stuff off, transferring items to a new list because the piece of paper was full. I decided I would only add items to the list that weren't part of my everyday life. Going to meetings and putting gas in the car joined brushing my teeth and taking a shower—they simply got done. I didn't have to list them. Other activities weren't so lucky.

As I modified the list, placing only out-of-the-ordinary tasks on it, I discovered two things: first, there was always something on the list, even when I removed my everyday tasks; second, there were items that remained on the list and that I didn't do.

One day, as I was adding something to my list, I found myself staring at it, reading and rereading it, wondering why I hadn't done some of the things I had listed. I took the paper, walked to my chair, sat down, and continued to go over the list. There were about ten things on the paper; ten seemed to be about the norm. There were three things, however, that had been on the list a very long time. I tried to remember when they had made the list, but couldn't. The best that I could recollect was "a few weeks ago." I scratched them off.

As soon as I scratched the items off the list without doing them, fear spoke up.

"*If you scratch them off without doing them, they may never get done,*" it said. "*Maybe not,*" I answered, "*but maybe they just aren't that important.*"

In that moment, I turned a corner in my lesson on patience. My lack of patience is based in fear. This illumination brought about a new way of looking at patience. I could clearly see patience was the overcoming of fear. When I am patient with myself, I have little fear about whether I will get things done or whether I have enough of whatever to get through life.

There will always be something on my list of things to do. There will always be items on my list of things I want or think I need; I finally came to grips with the notion that I had to learn to live with a full or partially full list of things to do or to get, whether they were material or spiritual. I could never completely finish those lists. Even if I did everything on my list of things to do in one day, and I did so more than once, I would continue to add to it, or start a new list the next day. This revelation allowed me to gain more patience with others. Before we go there, however, I want to say that my new attitude helped me practice a new lifestyle.

Today I do my best to do what I can. Then I let the rest go until later. I take time to relax and prepare—knowing that preparation is a large part of making something happen—and I do what I can do today. I let tomorrow create its own list and include the remainder of today's list, because it is going to do that anyway.

It was the thought "because it is going to do that anyway" that taught me how to have patience with other people. I had to change two words in my statement; I changed the wording to "because they are going to do that anyway." People are going to do what they are going to do. They don't ask for my input because they don't care what I might have to say about their day-to-day life. When it comes to people I don't know, forget about it; they are so far removed from my sphere of influence that I might as well try to blow out a forest fire as try to change what they do. Patience for other people comes from unconditional love. I must love them enough to let them be, to let them live their life without my input, unless they ask for it.

I must remind myself that they do things differently than I do, accept that they are not me—which is really a good thing, because I wouldn't want to live in a world filled only with people like me—and let them learn their own way, make their own mistakes, and do their own thing. I can do this with love; patience is a form of love, and love conquers fear.

When I quit giving my input if it wasn't asked for, the number of buttons I pushed dropped to almost zero. My acceptance that others will do what they are going to do allowed me to disconnect my own buttons so that even if people push them I won't react as I used to. I let them run their lives and I run mine. Sometimes I leave a situation with some anger at having my button pushed, or someone telling me how I need to do something, but I immediately begin to let it go by accepting that person as he or she is. This is a great way to practice patience with other people.

## Practice

I said it in my last book: I never did like to work at things. Practice, on the other hand, is fun. I found that doing the things necessary to change my life from the old way to this new, better-in-every-way life is easier if I consider what I am doing to be practice rather than work.

When I began recovery, it was work; I have to admit that. Changing so many bad habits at one time is hard; so is changing one bad habit that is so much a part of my life. When I quit using, however, colors looked brighter, things smelled better, life again had possibilities. In the beginning, making the necessary change was rather easy. Soon, however, I became used to the new look of the world. Then I had to work at making the changes necessary to maintain my joy and growth. I wasn't very happy about the fact that things got more difficult, but a quick talk with my sponsor helped me see the light at the end of the tunnel, and to know that it wasn't the train.

He told me that patience would go a long way toward helping me gain a better life. He also told me that I should focus on doing what was in front of me without worrying about how, when, or even if I would get the results I desired. He reminded me that the results I thought I needed might not be what I needed, that all my life I had been choosing my results, and things hadn't worked out in my favor; and maybe it was time to just do the work and let someone else determine the results for a while.

When I pointed out that doing the work wasn't really my idea of a good time, he said, "You shouldn't be looking for a good time, you should be looking for recovery, and working for it." I was not happy to hear this.

When I stumbled on the word practice at the end of the Twelfth Step, I found hope. My sponsor had told me I could borrow from the last three steps even during my early recovery, because they might help me avoid compounding old issues and creating new ones. The end of Step Twelve says we should "practice these principles in all our affairs." I got so excited that I never bothered to figure out what the principles were. I just wanted to practice instead of work. I took the idea to my sponsor. He thought for a few minutes, then nodded and said he thought it would be fine if I practiced instead of working—as long as I took my practice very seriously. I told him I would, and to this day, I do. Practicing the principles instead of working them has made the process of improvement much easier.

I remember going to meetings for about three weeks after our discussion about practicing the principles. We went to many step meetings. In a step meeting, one of the twelve steps of my recovery program is the topic of discussion. Of the many step meetings we attended, it seemed as though many focused on the Twelfth Step. I've noticed that coincidences seem to happen; when I need work in a particular area of my life, the topic of the meeting seems to be the same for a few meetings in a row. I notice this coincidence only if I pay attention.

We attended four or five meetings in a row (or so it seemed) where Step Twelve was the topic, and while I listened to people talk about helping other people or having a spiritual experience—which is also part of the step—all I wanted to talk about was practicing the principles in all my affairs. I felt like a big shot; I had something to talk about that no one else seemed to be very interested in. I was hitting on a part of the step that most people were overlooking. After two of these meetings, I was starting to think I was really on to something. People needed to hear what I had to say, or so I thought. After the third meeting, I knew I had something solid. I was the only person who even mentioned practicing the principles in all our affairs.

I was on a roll! Then lightning struck with the precision of a seasoned sharpshooter. After the fourth or fifth meeting focusing on Step Twelve—and after I had spouted off yet again about practicing the principles and thinking I had something nobody else had—it finally hit me. It rocked me to my core. This revelation didn't actually happen until we were on the way home after the meeting, and I am grateful that it didn't happen during the meeting. The experience was humbling, but if it had happened during the meeting, I might have been too humiliated to maintain my wits and learn the full lesson.

On the trip home, it dawned on me that I had no idea what the principles were. I had been running my mouth about practicing principles, which I thought was really the important part—but I didn't know what it was that I should be practicing. The principles I was talking about were suddenly in my face, and yet they were a mystery to me. I had never even stopped to think about what they might be, where I might find them, or even who might know what they were or where I could find them. I was baffled. "Oh my god!" I exclaimed.

"What?" floated from my sponsor's lips.

"I have been spouting off about practicing the principles for the last several meetings and I don't even know what they are!" My face reddened with embarrassment at the thought of my ignorance. The car was eerily silent for a moment. Then my sponsor cut the silence with his ever-so-inspiring words.

He said, "Looks like you have some work to do."

There was that word again. I hated work. I looked at him sideways. He was smiling. I knew the smile meant something, so I just kept my mouth shut and drove.

At first, I wanted to go back and fix my mistake—the one I had repeated meeting after meeting for over a week. Even though I knew that wasn't possible, it was the predominating thought in my head for several miles as traffic lights marked our progress. Finally, when I thought I would burst from the pressure, I looked over at my sponsor, noticed he was smiling at me, and said, "What am I going to do? I have to fix this. I spouted off about something I know nothing about."

"That's not entirely true," he said. Then he paused as I looked back and forth between him and the road. "You seem to understand practice pretty well. You just need to find out what the principles are, so you know what to practice."

All the air went out of me in a rush as I relaxed. I was saved. In the next breath, however, I thought I still needed to go back and change what I had said. I spoke about this, and he told me not to worry about it.

"There's always next week. And there's always another meeting on Step Twelve. You can do your homework and know more next time. That is what this program is all about, you know. Getting better is a long-term goal."

In the middle of my lesson on practice was a lesson in patience.

I looked at my hands and saw blood flowing back into them, the white knuckles growing pink as I relaxed my grip on the steering wheel. "Yeah, I've got some work to do," I agreed, suddenly anxious to get home to look up the principles. "If I am going to practice them, I should know what they are."

"I feel certain you will find them in short order. You can use that Internet thing you are always talking about; it seems to have a lot of information." Not having a computer, he had little idea just how valuable a tool the Internet is to the people who use it. He was nearly ninety when I met him, and he had never even owned an answering machine, let alone a computer. I thought, rather suddenly, that the Internet might have a lot of information, but it would never match his wisdom.

I dropped him off and left more quickly than normal, telling him I wanted to get home and get to work on those principles. He told me to be sure to let him know what I found out.

I found out a lot. The Internet is peppered with sites outlining principles, many of them corresponding to the twelve steps laid out in recovery programs.

I studied them and chose the ones I thought fit best. When I finished my research I felt better, and I went to bed feeling a little less foolish about the whole ordeal I had created.

The next day when I talked with my sponsor, I had my printout of the principles I had chosen from one of the sites that said they went along with the twelve steps. We discussed them, and he seemed satisfied that they would do just fine.

The principles I chose are as follows:

Step One, Acceptance; Step Two, Faith; Step Three, Surrender and Trust; Step Four, Honesty; Step Five, Courage; Step Six, Willingness; Step Seven, Humility; Step Eight, Forgiveness; Step Nine, Freedom; Step Ten, Perseverance; Step Eleven, Patience; Step Twelve, Charity and Love.

When we finished talking about them, I told him I planned to practice the principles to the best of my ability. He said that sounded like a lot of work. I laughed and said I would practice them.

I said, "Practice not only allows for mistakes, it alludes to the idea that I will make them. Work does not. Not in my mind."

"Just make sure that you practice them to the best of your ability," he said.

I promised I would, and I have to the best of my ability, which some days is pretty good and other days is not very good at all. Through it all, I have realized that a day of practicing the principles is a full day, and even though I am practicing, not *working*, the principles, it is a lot of work to change old habits into new ones. Still, I prefer to practice. It allows me more latitude.

One of the more important things I have learned while practicing the principles and changing my habits is that I am not my habits—I can change my habits. I used to think that habits were impossible to change. While sometimes it may seem like it's impossible to change a habit, I know with perseverance, with continued effort, I can do it. That saying about not being able to teach an old dog new tricks is false. I can change if I want to.

In the beginning, it may take hard work to begin the change, but after a while I can practice the new habit and it will eventually replace the old one. I have done it enough times now to know that it happens every time I am serious enough about wanting to change.

I like working on myself, I like making me better, and I like helping other people change for the better too when they ask. Because what I am working on is always changing, the work is always new and exciting, even if it is work. Although I still tend toward practice whenever I can use it instead of work, which is usually after I have done at least some work, I do not see work the way I used to. I realized that I disliked the routine of work. It wasn't the work, but rather the routine or the repetition of something I didn't want to do that I disliked. Calling it practice makes it more palatable, but it doesn't change the nature of the beast.

I still call it practice when I can, because practice allows for mistakes, but I am not against doing the work that helps me define what I need to practice.

## Problems

"We are continually faced with great opportunities brilliantly disguised as impossible problems."

I saw the quote on my psychologist friend's wall in his office. I liked it immediately because my sponsor always told me that there are no problems, only opportunities. This quote drove home the point that opportunities are disguised as problems. They are so well hidden, in fact, that I can miss them altogether if I am not looking carefully. Fear keeps me from looking carefully at it.

I have learned to believe that problems arise from fear. Problems generally surface in the form of fear that I will lose something I have or not get something I want. When I have a problem rather than an opportunity, I have found that it is fear that keeps me from seeing the opportunities that may lie within. Each problem carries with it at least one opportunity for personal, emotional, or spiritual growth. It is up to me to find the opportunity under the disguise, to find the diamond in the rough. I can do this by facing the fear, seeing it for what it is, and moving through it.

For example, when I got into recovery, I thought I had a drinking problem. Then I discovered I had a stopping problem—and a living, coping, problem-solving, perception, and emotional problem. I was fraught with problems. For a long time I lived in these problems, struggling to find a way out. When my sponsor pointed out that there are no problems, only opportunities, I began looking for the opportunities hidden within the problems. Soon I began to see them.

I used for twenty-five years, give or take, and while they weren't all bad years, drinking and drugging didn't cause me serious trouble until near the end. As I look back, I can see that things could have been better if I had done things differently. I began to see my life as a series of problems caused by alcohol and other drugs. My biggest regret became the fact that I used for so much of my life. When I began looking for the opportunities that may have been lying hidden in these problems, the opportunities began to surface.

For starters, I saw that if I was able to humble myself enough to make an example of myself of what not to do, I could use my long using career to show young people in the program that staying in recovery was a good thing. I began helping young people as best I could, and God provided me with many opportunities to do so. I have sponsored many young people since I decided my life could be used as an example of how using is a poor way to spend time.

As I humbled myself enough to see my life as a shining example of what *not* to do, I began to see other opportunities to use my experiences to help others. I flunked out of college when I was young because I hated school. I didn't want to be there, so I quit. I got a job I didn't like because it paid well, and I stayed in that job even though I didn't like it and knew I had more potential, and ended up making a career of it. I was afraid of everything. Since I didn't know better, I ran from the fear, and every time I ran I ended up at the bottom of a bottle or bag of dope. These weren't good examples of how to live life, but I discovered that even a bad example can serve the greater good if used properly.

While I possessed some humility, what really had to happen was that I had to get humble enough to admit that there were problems, and then I had to find the opportunities.

While talking to a friend one day, I found words coming out of my mouth that made perfect sense. I was listening to myself as I told my friend that she needed to overcome her issues in order to help others. I said, in effect, that she needed to deal with her issues because someday someone would come into her life who needed help with the same things she was dealing with. I told her that if she had dealt with her issues properly, she would be able to help this person, and if she hadn't, she would lose the chance to make a difference in this other person's life.

As the words made their way from my mouth to my ears, I knew God was talking to me as much as I was talking to this woman. I had to overcome my issues as well if I was ever going to be of service to others who had issues to deal with similar to mine. As I have overcome my problems—my living, coping, problem-solving, perception, and emotional problems—I have become better able to help others with similar issues. There were opportunities right in front of me; I simply had to seize them.

Since that day, and especially since I gathered enough humility to admit my faults, I have been able to see the opportunities that lie within my problems. I have overcome many of my faults and shortcomings, and I can help others by showing them how I did it.

This book and *Becoming Normal* are perfect examples of problems turned into opportunities. I share my experience and struggles, as well as the solutions and opportunities I have gained from them, with others in the form of books in the hope that everyone who reads them will find a way to deal with their own faults and shortcomings.

If I hadn't lived the life I had, I wouldn't be able to share these insights. I wouldn't have the experiences I have to offer. Today I thank God for all of my past problems and the fear that went with them, because I have something to offer others who might be struggling as I have struggled.

When I was younger I heard someone say, "Live every day as though it were your last." I decided that I wanted to finish my bucket list, but I found my bucket was full of crap. It took a long time to make this discovery, but I know it now, and today I do my best to fill my bucket list with things that are helpful, and not harmful to me or the people around me. Most importantly, I keep my old bucket list around because it is a good list of what not to do—so I can show it to other people. I want to be able to do that so I can show how I overcame or am overcoming problems by turning them into opportunities.

The last thing I want to say about problems is this: If I have a problem with you, it is still my problem and not yours. I have the problem. I mentioned this in *Becoming Normal*, but I think it bears repeating. After all, I seem to get most angry when I am wrong or when I have a problem with you, and I tend to believe this is due to my fear. All too often, I have a problem with someone else because he is right and I am wrong and all I can see is the problem in front of me. People do not get mad when you lie about them; they get mad when you tell the truth about them. When I am wrong and it is the truth and I do not want to believe it, that is a problem. I have found that I can remove the problem by looking for my opportunity for growth. Problems are full of negative energy by nature; opportunities are full of positive energy. If I can encase myself in the positive, I not only dilute the negative or eliminate it; I live in the solution rather than "suffering" in the problem. I believe this is a necessity today—to live in the positive energy produced by looking for opportunities and solutions rather than looking for a way to blame others for my situation. The simple process of doing this lessens the amount of fear or potential fear that I have to deal with in my life.

## Program

When I decided that I might need a program to recover from my addiction, I fell prey to fear. I was afraid of several things in the beginning, and although I mention them here in relation to joining a twelve-step program, they are fears that try to permeate my life to this day. The fears I am talking about involved change. For starters, I was afraid that if I joined a program and quit my addiction, I would become less of a person. I would be giving up a part of my life—one I had enjoyed for years even though it had caused me trouble—and I wasn't sure I would be able to replace the enjoyment I had gotten out of my using with what came from a program.

I feel it is important to say here that while I did enjoy using for several years, toward the end it was anything but fun. Once my addiction grabbed me—once my "friends" turned on me—the fun was over. If things had still been fun, I probably wouldn't have quit. I know myself well enough to say that today. I simply wouldn't have quit if things hadn't gotten so bad that the fear of living as I was outweighed the fear of joining a program. However, that didn't make the fear of joining a program any less difficult or any easier to overcome.

There were actually two fears working against each other. One was the fear of getting into recovery; the other was the fear of not getting into recovery. One might say I was afraid to change and afraid to stay the same. Still, something had to change. Staying the same wasn't working for me. Without knowing it, I used fear as a tool and chose to change. I joined a program.

When I first joined my fellowship, I didn't have a sponsor or friends who could tell me what I was in for or be of any real help, at least not at first. In the very beginning, I considered that a treatment center—a rehab facility—was an unnecessary stigma to attach to myself. The only thing looming larger than my fear was my humiliation at the thought of being branded a loser.

Fortunately, the pain of continuing on the path of self-destruction was more than I could bear, and I decided to get the help I would need to get things started.

Sometimes pain is what it takes to make a change that I desperately need to make. This is especially true when I have little or no support, or sense that I have no support. Fear can seem the most dangerous when I have, or think I have, little help available. Even when I know what I need to do, it can seem impossible to do it because if I fail I will have no one to help me or, in my twisted way of thinking, have no one else to blame for the failure.

So the pain and fear of remaining the same pressed me into making a change I didn't want to make, even though I had no idea what I was getting into and no idea what I might get out of it. I didn't know what this program, this fellowship, might make of me or make me do. As I became more afraid of what I might become, I ran many haunting scenarios through my head. None of them seemed to be happy, fun, or exciting ways of moving forward. I knew I would become boring at best, and impossible to be around at worst. I would never be happy again, let alone free to do what I wanted to do. I would have to do what other people told me to do, what a program told me to do, and I had never really done that before. I wasn't looking forward to being told what to do. All my life I had rebelled at authority, structure, and routine.

As usual, I knew little about what the future held.

As I spent my time in treatment, I began to learn some things; when I left treatment, although the fear seemed to grow when I left the protected environment, I was beginning to see some positive changes materialize in my life. Slowly but surely, a couple of good things happened. I noticed I was freer than when I went into treatment. I didn't have to use anymore, and since I didn't have to use like I did when I went in, I could make other good choices. That was a freeing discovery. Of course, choice presented problems of its own, because I was so used to being told what to do by alcohol and drugs (even though I didn't realize it until I got clean) that I didn't know how to make good decisions by myself. Fear jumped all over this revelation, using it to try to get me to go back to my addiction. My fear told me that even as uncomfortable as addiction was, I knew what to expect. I knew that was true to some extent, but I also knew that I did all sorts of things I never expected when I was using. Even my active addiction had become something unpredictable. I couldn't—I wouldn't—go back to that.

Instead, I decided to trust what I had learned in treatment. I would seek out a program and hope to find help there. I heard there was help in the fellowship, and I decided to have a look before I ran back to the old methods.

I would love to say that I did it all right the first time, but I didn't. I met my first sponsor three days out of treatment and I asked him to be my sponsor two days later. He agreed, and we got to work—or at least he did.

I thought I was doing well, and I did not use for eight months. Then one day, after dropping my sponsor off after a meeting and heading home for the night, I stopped and bought a pint of Jack Daniel's. I figured I would have just one drink and nurse the bottle over the weekend. Before I finished the fifteen-minute trip home, I had nearly polished off the pint. Instead of going straight home, I stopped at another liquor store and bought a fifth.

This last slip led me to a three-month-long spree resulting in my second trip to treatment in less than a year. I spent eight months in recovery, and I went out for three months.

Fortunately, it also led me to the conclusions I needed to make in order to finally decide I could no longer "drink like a gentleman." In fact, I could not drink at all, not successfully and not socially.

My second trip to treatment was more humbling than humiliating, more relaxed than fear-ridden. I went in with a more open mind. I knew I had "missed something" the first time around, and I wanted to find out what it was.

I had tasted recovery, and it was good. The eight months I had was better than I thought it would be. When I went back to treatment, I did my best to open my mind and learn. I was particularly looking for the key, the thing I had missed. Looking back, I can say it was painfully obvious. At the time, however, it eluded me completely. Finally, it hit me between the eyes.

Fear was the culprit. I was afraid that people would not like me if they knew I needed a program in order to live. The idea that people would think less of me, or worse, laugh at me behind my back, for being less of a person made me afraid. Because of my fear, I had never grasped the principle of the First Step in recovery—acceptance. I had not accepted the fact that I was different, that I always will be different from other people. I still struggled with the idea that I would never be able to use socially the way I saw some of my friends do. As I struggled with this revelation, I was struggling with my addiction. When I fight my addiction, I lose. I had to rid myself of the fear woven into the idea of being different, the idea that I should be able to— somehow, someday—drink like other people.

Acceptance was a strange beast when I first met it. At least it felt that way to me. I was introduced to acceptance in a rather unusual way. A girl in treatment said, "Acceptance is knowing you are an addict and being okay with that fact."

That simple sentence struck me hard. I realized in an instant that I had been fighting, and losing, a battle with wanting things to be different. I wanted to not be an alcoholic. I wanted it because I thought other people would think less of me if I didn't. I learned later that what other people think is up to them, not me, and I learned that what I think other people think is nothing more than what I think.

I set out to accept the fact that I was always going to be different. To be okay with that fact and to let others be as they wished was my challenge. I decided that before I left treatment that last time, I needed to completely accept this fact if I was to get better.

Gradually, over the two weeks I was in treatment, I found acceptance.

In my first real attempt at getting into recovery, I thought somehow I would graduate from the program and become like everybody else. I thought one day I would be cured of my disease. What I discovered was that I wouldn't graduate out of the fellowship—I would graduate into it.

When I got out of treatment that second time, I went to my sponsor and told him I was ready to do what I needed to do. I stopped asking why he wanted me to do things and just did them. I began to learn. One of the biggest lessons I learned is that it takes a lot of work to change from a life of active addiction to a life of recovery.

There is a path running alongside each of the Twelve Steps. I can choose to take the path, or to move up a step. Moving up takes energy. Staying on the same path, while requiring less work, makes for little progress. To overcome the fears I carried, I had to get off the level path of my old thinking and move up the steps.

As I began to embrace the program and the fellowship, and I began to quit worrying about what other people might think of me, I began to grow. I began to overcome some of my fears, and I started to see that, for the most part, people were rooting for me to succeed. They weren't hoping I would fail. They didn't think less of me—or at least they didn't say that.

As I began to see the truth, my fear of what others thought began to disappear. As I started to be more useful to my fellows in the program, as well as to society in general, the fear slipped away even more.

Today I am a productive member of society, and as long as I don't use or act out, I can be as normal and as helpful as anyone can be. When I look at it this way, when I see using as my only stumbling block, I can see that I really have it pretty good.

There are no outward deformities, no crutches to carry around, and no sign on my forehead. There is nothing to distinguish me from anybody else in society—as long as I don't use and do what I am supposed to.

Because I am in a program, I must carry the message just as I used to carry the woes of the world—constantly, and inside me. I found the message in the principles of the program. They were daunting at first—a long list of seemingly impossible principles I needed to live by: acceptance, faith, surrender, trust, honesty, courage, willingness, humility, forgiveness, freedom, perseverance, patience, charity and love.

I like to say that if I ever get them all right on any given day, I want to die that day so that I can go out on a winning streak. Of course, I am kidding, but it goes to show that I know it is a lofty goal. Still, I strive for this goal today because I also know it makes me a better person just by doing my best to live by them even if I don't get it completely right. In doing my best to live by these principles, I am carrying the message of the program to others.

While I do my best to live by the principles just for my benefit, I also do so because when people find out I am in the program, they may judge the program through me. If they happen to be someone who needs recovery, or even if they know someone who does, and I show them a poor example of what the program can do, I might be the reason they decide not to try recovery. That is the worst thing I can think of: me being the reason someone doesn't get into recovery. However, that is really the least of the reasons I like to practice the principles of the program.

My favorite reason for practicing the principles is that it makes me a better person. It makes me the person I liked to think I was when I was using—on a roll, and with an answer for everything. Practicing the principles helps me see that I don't have all the answers, that I don't need to have them, and that I can still be a good, helpful person even though I don't know everything.

As I graduated into the program, I also learned that it can be a lifesaver or a life creator.

If I see it as a lifesaver, I will limit myself to less than the program and life afford. When I started seeing it as a life creator, I began putting forth the effort necessary to begin enjoying life. Getting into recovery was just the beginning of my journey. It saved my life, and I won't deny that. However, after a while it created in me a desire for more, a desire I didn't know what to do with at first.

I talked to my sponsor and he suggested, as he did on many occasions, that I pray about it. I started praying, and answers came. If I wanted more out of life, I had to put more into life. I had to walk through the fear that kept me from doing the things needed to create a new life, instead of just not using and moving forward in the same old way—full of fear and misery—just having my life, not living it.

I have learned that I need to put principles first in my life if I want to grow. If I want to live with the principles mentioned earlier, they must become a part of every waking hour. The only way I know to do that is to do my best to live them. The only way I know to do that is to practice them constantly. Even when I don't want to practice them—especially when I don't want to—I must practice whatever it is I want to become.

I made a list of the principles and kept it handy so I would know what I was supposed to be practicing. I looked up the words in the dictionary and wrote them down as well. I thought about them a lot. I focused on their meaning and what it meant to live my life based on those principles. I have become pretty good at living life based upon the principles given to me by the program.

Putting principles before personalities—including my own—has helped me practice the principles to the point where they are becoming a large part of my personality. I never get them all completely right in a given day. I am still human and I still get mad, feel fear, and say stupid things, but I do my best to practice today what I want to be tomorrow.

The program was nothing to fear, even though it seemed like it was. Most things are like that. Fear stands there and tells me I can't do it, I won't like it, or people will think I am crazy. Fear tells me whatever it thinks I need to hear to stop me from reaching my goals. Fear, however, is a liar, one I must stop believing if I am to continue to grow.

# 11 | Giving, Living, Gratitude, and Growth

I used to wonder how I deserved all this. How is it that I managed to find recovery when so many seem unable to do so? How was I chosen to receive the gift of recovery? What did I do to deserve this wonderful new life?

These questions plagued me in early recovery. I brought the questions up to my sponsor. He paused, looked me squarely in the eye, and, very quietly yet sternly, said, "When are you going to quit asking, 'Why me?'"

I chewed on that for a moment and decided he had a point. All my life I had been asking "Why me?" The big difference here was that I was asking why good things were happening instead of the bad things that always seemed to happen when I was using. As I thought this through, I could tell there was more. His eyes never left mine, and although my mind was moving at breakneck speed, I kept my mouth shut and waited for what he had to say next. He folded his hands, formed his index fingers into a steeple, and rested his chin on them. I watched, anticipating.

"I'll bet when you were using, you spread your misery with everything you did. Maybe not on purpose, of course, but you couldn't help but share negativity when you had so much of it." He paused again, this time for effect, then added, "Why don't you just go out and give away some of this newfound recovery, this new way of life, this happiness? Instead of turning such a wonderful, positive thing into a negative, why don't you go give it away? Spread it like you used to spread your misery—everywhere."

I was stunned. The questions came back. What did I have to offer? I decided to give it some thought before I asked the question.

As I studied the thought of giving away what I had—and what I might have to give to begin with—one idea rushed to the forefront of my mind and stayed there.

In the past, I had always given with an agenda. I had always looked for what I might get in return for what I gave. In giving away my recovery, I could find nothing that I could gain. I had heard in meetings that we must "give it away to keep it," but I still wasn't familiar with how that worked—I was still new to the whole concept. But I decided to give it a try.

Fear, fueled by my diseased thinking, told me that if I gave away what I had, I wouldn't have it anymore and I would relapse again. I didn't want that. My confusion led me back to my sponsor.

After letting out a snort of laughter, he said, "If you don't use, you can't relapse. You aren't giving away your recovery, you are giving away the things you have learned that help you not to use. And you aren't really giving it away, so to speak; you are *sharing* it."

I calmed down a little and decided to try it. I learned a lot.

I received a handout one time that said we remember 10 percent of what we read, 20 percent of what we hear, 30 percent of what we see, 50 percent of what we see and hear, 70 percent of what we discuss with others, 80 percent of what we personally experience, and 95 percent of what we teach others. I have no idea how accurate those figures are, but I noticed that what we seem to learn the best is what we teach. Teaching, I reasoned, is a form of giving. Giving must be a good way to learn even the things I already know. I must already know them at least a little in order to teach them to someone else. This, I surmised, is the reality behind giving it away to keep it. When I help someone else, I reinforce it in myself.

Giving became much easier after that little revelation. I began giving what little I had, and to my surprise, I watched what I had to offer grow. Soon the fear, which had tried to talk me out of the idea, was bowing to my newly discovered confidence. I was freely giving what I had to others, and it not only felt good, it did good, and it helped me as much as, and sometimes more than, it helped those I was giving to. I was doing good things.

Then a new fear cropped up. *If I continue to do good, people will come to expect it from me all the time*, I thought. *There is no way I can do good all the time for the rest of my life* followed that, and I became afraid that I was setting myself up for a fall. I went back to my sponsor. He always seemed to have the right answer, even if I was not ready to hear it. "Of course there is no way you can do good all the time," he said. "You are human. You will make mistakes—some may be horrible, damaging, catastrophic mistakes." Then he smiled as I frowned, and added, "But you know what to do when that happens, right?"

"No," I blurted. "I have no idea."

"Sure you do," he said. "It is laid out in the program. You make amends. You change. You learn. You grow. You move on."

I thought on that for a while before I stumbled upon a saying by Henry Ford that says, "...Failure is only the opportunity to more intelligently begin again." I first saw this quote on one of those saying-a-day calendars that my mother gets me every year for Christmas. The saying happened to be on my birthday, which struck me as some kind of sign. I posted the small page on my refrigerator and did my best to give this thought a home in my head. Today I reword it for my own use, as I often do. I know it today as this: Failure is but an opportunity to more intelligently begin again. A subtle change, for sure, but it fits me better if I think of it this way. I remind myself that failure is not the end. It is but a beginning.

When I give of myself, I will make mistakes, and sometimes I will fail. That doesn't, however, have to end my giving. In fact, knowing that I will make mistakes and be able to correct them, learn for myself, and grow is a great reason for giving. This is especially true when I couple it with the understanding that teaching or giving is the best way for me to learn.

It is a wonderful thing to go to a meeting and get something out of it, but it is even better to go to meetings in order to give and to give what I have to offer for others to pick up or leave behind. Not everyone will agree with what I have to say or the example I offer with my life, but by sharing what I have, at the very least I reinforce it within myself.

Occasionally, I even find that I say something I no longer agree with. I know that sounds funny, but the truth of the matter is that as I grow, I change, and as I change, I sometimes realize that I don't believe things I used to believe. One great example of this is that I used to believe using was not harmful to either myself or those around me. Even after I got into recovery, I thought for too long that I hadn't harmed other people with my antics because I used mostly at home, away from other people. Today I know better. Since I changed how I feel about that, why shouldn't I be open to changing how I feel about other things in life?

One of the biggest things I have changed is that today I give without looking for what I might get back. I have overcome the fear that told me I might not get back as much as I put forth. I have done this through doing. I give whenever I can. Somehow, I always seem to get back at least as much as I give. In the meantime, I am not wasting time and energy trying to figure out something I can't figure out—namely, what will I get out of this? Fear is what told me I needed to know, but fear is a liar, a cheat, and a fraud.

## Gratitude

When it comes to disabling fear, gratitude is an amazing weapon. I have discovered that gratitude can spoil fear faster than almost anything else can. Gratitude helps me live in the moment, and when I live in the moment, I always have enough.

Right this minute I have enough of everything I need to go on, and since fear is nearly always based on losing something I have or not getting something I want, if I live in the here and now, fear cannot bother me.

I heard it put a funny way once. Someone said, "Just be a Who."

They were talking about the Whos in Whoville in the Dr. Seuss story *How the Grinch Stole Christmas*. When the Grinch stole all the presents, the tree trimmings, and even the food, the Whos didn't get mad or fill themselves with fear; instead they sang. They all met in the town center, held hands around the tree, and sang. They were grateful for what they had, not afraid of what they might have missed or wouldn't get.

While this may be a funny children's story, the lesson is clear. If I can maintain my gratitude for the things I have, I will have to deal with fear a lot less. I will have enough, and I will be able to sing instead of pouting or feeling fear and anger.

I used to look for instant gratification. Now I look for instant gratitude. I consciously look for all the good things I have in this life that make it so wonderful. There are enough bad, even horrific, things going on in the world to cause me to freeze up and sink into despair if I allow them to. The goal is to not allow the bad things in life to get me down, because when I get down I can fall prey to fear, anger, and loathing. However, if I fill myself with gratitude, I can focus on the good things in life and move toward a better way of thinking and living.

Being mindful of the moment helps me to be more grateful. Spending my time focused on the present moment helps me live my life, as I should, in the here and right now. I want to be happy now, not later. I want to have love now, and not wait. To have these things I must bring them into my life.

To bring what I want into my life, I must give the same to others. If I want love, I must give love. If I want a friend, I must be a friend.

A friend once told me that you can't give a hug without getting one back. I have discovered that the same is true for many other good things in life. I must give them to get them. Somehow showing gratitude seems to bring more of it into my life. When I practice being grateful, I get better at it. It feels good when I practice it, so I do it as often as I can.

## Growth

Growth is not about how I feel. If I only did things that felt good, I would limit my activity and growth. I used to focus on doing what felt good at the time. That got me into a lot of trouble because it fed my disease. I wanted to feel good now—right now—all the time. That is not the way to grow, and I have learned that I want growth over just feeling good. I want it for a very good reason, too. Growth feels good. It may take longer than popping a pill, smoking a joint, drinking a pint, or acting out in one of many other destructive ways.

It may take a lot more work, too. However, once I am on the road to growth, the growth itself feels good. And once I am growing more than not, I feel good more often than not. I must remember that new growth can be hard, at least at first, but soon the hard work pays off and I begin nurturing a new habit that feels much better than anything I used to do to feel good.

It lasts longer, too, and while I am at it, fear seems to fade away and leave me alone.

To grow, I must step outside myself and do what is right instead of what I like or what makes me feel good. The process of growth can bring on fear; however, if I face the fear, I can overcome it and change into a better, happier person. Since overcoming fear is the goal, I need to meet fear and some painful situations head-on in order to move into a more fun and productive future.

"Growth has a price," my first sponsor liked to say.

When I asked him what the price was, he said it varies. "One can lie in bed and grow old, or one can get out of bed and move about. Even that has a price, albeit a small one."

As we talked about growth, I came to see that he was right. Going back to school was a major undertaking for me. There was a lot of fear and mental anguish at first, but after a while, I was growing. I moved right through the pain and fear. I simply put forth the effort, paid the price, and met my goal.

The same is true for any undertaking. There is a price to pay monetarily, mentally, physically, emotionally; you name it, there is a price to pay, and the price varies based upon the amount of growth possible. Like anything in life, the greater the payoff, the higher the price.

With growth, though, I cannot put it on a charge card and pay the bill later. I have to pay the price of admission up front, as I go, in order to receive a desirable outcome. There are times when I discover that I have put my growth on a virtual charge card. When I make a mistake, growth is possible, but only if I am willing to learn from my mistakes. When life smacks me upside the head for seemingly no reason at all, I grow as well. Sometimes this backwards way of growing hurts—sometimes it hurts a lot. However, if I am willing to learn from the pain, I will eventually grow. I used to think that growing meant giving myself over to someone else's way of thinking or doing things. I thought it meant giving up control of my life. It's not about giving up control;

it's about learning to use my control in a positive manner. I must learn to do the *right* thing, not the *easy* thing. God helps me see and do the right thing, and accomplish it too. When I give my control over to God, He gives it back, but He usually gives it back with a suggestion or a hint of what to do. I believe we call that free will. When I am willing and able to listen to that still, small voice that speaks from within and use my power of deduction to figure out what is right and what is wrong, I can usually make the proper choices in life.

I usually run my ideas past my sponsor, a friend, or a family member before I take action if I am the least bit concerned about making the choice, but in the end the choice is mine.

No matter what choice I make, there are consequences to deal with. Sometimes they are good consequences, other times they are not. In coping with these consequences, I grow and learn to make even better choices, experience better consequences, and grow in the future. The key is to do the next right thing, to the best of my ability, while letting God take care of what is to come next. I can make choices and take actions, but the results are not up to me. When I can let go and let God take care of results, I know I have grown.

## Living

Living can be as fun, or as burdensome, as I want to make it. Life can be happiness or sadness, love or anger, courage or fear. The choice is mine.

I have heard it said that "life is 10 percent what happens to me and 90 percent how I react to it." I tend to take "what happens to me" and remove the "to me" part, because when I think things happen "to me" I tend to put myself in the victim role. I used to spend too much time thinking I was a victim of other people's actions, of giant corporations, of alcohol and drugs. Today I refuse to play the victim role. I say, "Life is 10 percent what happens and 90 percent how I react to it." I'm not crazy about the "react" part of the saying, either. Today I like to see life as a series of actions, life happenings, and consequences. Then I act on those consequences. Even when something does happen to me, I prefer to think of myself as acting on what I have to deal with instead of reacting to it. I think my dislike for the word react has to do with my old knee-jerk reactions from my past. Because these types of reactions didn't work too well back then, I do my best nowadays to avoid reacting to life's challenges.

I can't find a way to remove the word react from the "10 percent/90 percent" quotation above because all too often I do have to react to life, to what others say and do, to what companies or other institutions do, and to the challenges that life seems to throw my way. I have to act on or react to the consequences caused by some person, place, or thing that isn't me. These are certainly reactions, because I didn't do or cause the initial action. Not too amazingly, these are just the situations where fear likes to rear its ugly head.

What will somebody else do to disrupt my life? What will I have to do to bail myself out of someone else's mess or the mess someone else caused? How will some action reported on the news affect me? This list of questions about life's ups and downs can be endless, and the misery heaped upon me can be insurmountable. However, I do not have to let it get to me. Today I do my best to live in the now, to enjoy the moment, to take life one thing at a time. I don't multitask; I don't even try to. I see multitasking as more stress than it's worth. Besides, I have discovered that when I do multitask, I tend to make more mistakes, mistakes that I will need to fix later. I would rather put forth my best effort the first time and get it right, or as close as I can to right, the first time around.

I refuse to let other people push me or prod me into doing things I don't want to do, unless they have the authority to do so, of course, and even then I make it known that I am against the idea. I say no when I feel the need to recenter, relax, or take care of me.

I have learned that in taking care of me, I can then take care of others. If I neglect myself in order to take care of others, soon I am in need of the support of others instead of being in a position to help them.

I still ask for help when I need it, and I need plenty of it. What I do to the best of my ability is take my time. I need time to take care of me, to do what I need to do to stay sane and happy so that when others need me, I am useful.

A perfect example is when I can't find my car keys because I am frazzled and in a hurry. I try to remember to stop for a moment and relax so I can think, act, or react to a situation more calmly and more lovingly.

I need my breaks. I think everyone does. Some need more breaks than others do, and I have discovered that I am one who needs a lot of downtime. This need for downtime is still no excuse for not getting things done. Not getting things done is a cause of fear, so I must get things done. I don't have to get everything done today. I certainly don't have to get everything done today by sacrificing my time for relaxing. Skipping breaks makes me less productive and more fearful of not getting things done.

It may sound counterproductive, but taking a break can often help me get finished, just like in the previous example where I am trying to find my car keys. When I let my brain relax, it can think. When I can think more clearly, I make better choices; when I make better choices, the consequences are better. When people say I'm too young, or too old, or just too plain crazy to act like they think I should, I have to remember that only I can make my own choices. In fact, if I choose not to make a choice, I still have made a choice. If I abdicate my choice to someone else, I have chosen to do so. Therefore, when I choose, I must do so carefully. It is my life that I am choosing, one choice at a time.

Some choices are easy, but many are difficult. Some are very difficult, and bring fear in massive quantities. Since living with fear is inevitable, I figure it is time I learn how to do it well.

Today I do my best to use fear as a tool; I use it to remind myself when there is something that I must correct or adjust. More often than not, the thing that needs correcting or adjusting is in me, although sometimes others need to change. I must accept that things will get better when they do or stay bad or even get worse, for as long as they don't. Either way, I can only do my part, yet I *must* do my part, and I must do my part with courage and conviction.

As I walk through, or knock down, the walls of fear that crop up in my life, I become better at it, and the walls become smaller, weaker, and easier to walk through or knock down. Sometimes I just need to keep it that simple. I need to remember that fear is just part of the process.